WEAVING
THE CRADLE

'This book is a treasure trove of inspiring work with parents and babies in groups. I was impressed by the honesty and reflectiveness of the diverse facilitators and families who reveal their feelings of anxiety, disappointment, irritation and joy, their mistakes and successes. If only there were such powerfully supportive groups in every neighbourhood.'

– Dr Sue Gerhardt, author of Why Love Matters, *co founder of OXPIP (Oxford Parent Infant Project)*

'Here we have a real dynamo of a book which pumps out the energy, commitment and skills of all its contributors. This overview of the many different ways therapeutic groups can provide help and support to vulnerable parents who may be struggling to manage with their baby, or apprehensive about the baby to be, is an inspiration to all those who engage with such parents. This is preventative intervention at its most inventive.

Those who work in children's centres, will find this a resource full of the different communities they serve and are so central to. This is relationship-based practice at its best.'

– Robin Balbernie, Consultant Child Psychotherapist, Infant Mental Health Specialist, Clinical Director of PIP UK

'This is just the sort of record we need of the work done by children's centres and their partners, and the outcomes achieved through this work.'

– Karen Walker, Centre Manager, North & North West Abingdon Children's Centres

'This inspiring book has been skilfully woven by Monika Celebi with the same loving care that each chapter author shows towards the parents and their babies. Indeed a triumph of collaboration, clear writing with great depth, and a joy to read.'

– Hilary Kennedy, Educational Psychologist CPsychol, AFBPsS, Video Interaction Guidance (AVIGuk) Practitioner, Supervisor

'This valuable manual for practitioners acknowledges that mothering poses both wondrous moments and difficult challenges, especially when baby care reactivates unprocessed visceral residues. Chapters illustrate how multi-faceted 'attachment-based' group interventions increase parental sensitivity, empathy, and mentalization, delivered across venues and continents.'

– Joan Raphael-Leff, Psychoanalyst/Transcultural Psychologist and Leader, Academic Faculty for Psychoanalytic Research, Anna Freud Centre, London

WEAVING
THE CRADLE

Facilitating Groups to Promote
Attunement and Bonding between
Parents, Their Babies and Toddlers

Edited by Monika Celebi
with Rebecca Foster
Foreword by Jane Barlow

 SINGING
DRAGON

LONDON AND PHILADELPHIA

First published in 2017
by Singing Dragon
an imprint of Jessica Kingsley Publishers
73 Collier Street
London N1 9BE, UK
and
400 Market Street, Suite 400
Philadelphia, PA 19106, USA

www.singingdragon.com

Library of Congress Cataloging in Publication Data
Names: Celebi, Monika, editor.
Title: Weaving the cradle : facilitating groups to promote attunement and
   bonding between parents, their babies and toddlers / edited by Monika
   Celebi ; foreword by Jane Barlow.
Description: London ; Philadelphia : Singing Dragon, 2017. | Includes
   bibliographical references and index.
Identifiers: LCCN 2016056001 | ISBN 9781848193116 (alk. paper)
Subjects: LCSH: Parent and child--Psychological aspects. | Parent-infant
   psychotherapy. | Group psychotherapy. | Attachment behavior.
Classification: LCC BF723.P25 .W38 2017 | DDC 362.82/86--dc23 LC record
available at https://lccn.loc.gov/2016056001

British Library Cataloguing in Publication Data
A CIP catalogue record for this book is available from the British Library

ISBN 978 1 84819 311 6
eISBN 978 0 85701 264 7

Printed and bound in Great Britain

I dedicate this book to my children Robin and Sulia
who taught me how wonderful and how challenging it is to be a mother.

Contents

Foreword

'Weaving' is the process of bringing together threads to produce new and interesting phenomena, and 'cradles' are of course the traditional baskets or beds in which babies are nursed through their earliest days. *Weaving the Cradle*, as the rather wonderful title of this book suggests, is not, however, about weaving a physical space, but more fundamentally about the complex processes involved in developing a containing mind not only for the baby but for the parent as well, through the use of groups to deliver some new and exciting methods of parenting support.

The need for a containing mind originates in the work of Bion (1962) who, as part of his theory of thinking, talked about 'alpha' and 'beta' elements, and the need for all babies to have access to an 'alpha function'. His theory suggests that beta elements, which are best thought of as the raw or unmetabolized aspects of experience that emerge from the mind, body and feelings, need to be turned into alpha elements, which are processed experiences that can be thought about (Bion 1962). Bion believed that the mother provides this 'alpha function' for her baby in a variety of ways such as through her capacity for reverie, and her ability to tolerate and modify the baby's distress. And there is now a rapidly developing body of research demonstrating the importance of the primary caregiver's ability to do this for the baby, in terms of the young child's later capacity for emotion regulation (e.g. Meins *et al.* 2001, 2012), which is now recognized to be the foundation of later mental health (Fonagy 2001).

This book focuses on the use of groups to support parents both before and following the birth of their baby, which is a key window of opportunity to promote the wellbeing of the parent-baby dyad, not only because of the high motivation of parents to do the best at this time, but because of the sensitivity of the unborn/newborn baby's brain to environmental input, and in particular to interactions with their primary caregivers (Schore 2001).

The use of groups to support parents began back in the 1960s when it was recognized that the then largely behavioural parent training programmes being developed to help parents manage difficult child behaviour could be developed just as effectively, and possibly more cost-effectively, using groups. Five decades later, the use of groups to deliver parenting programmes has become the norm, and there is recognition that the opportunity to meet with other parents at key points in the child's development has benefits that derive in part from the experience of being in a group with other parents. Indeed, a recent systematic review of studies that had explored parents' views about group-based parent-training programmes found that it was the increased feelings of acceptance and support from other parents in the group, in addition to factors such as increased knowledge, skills and understanding, that enabled parents to regain control and feel more able to cope (Kane, Wood and Barlow 2007). The chapters in this book suggest that in fact groups may have an important alpha function for parents.

This book does not, however, focus on the use of groups to deliver standard parent training programmes; rather, it explores their use to deliver innovative methods of working with the parent-baby dyad during the perinatal period, including many that are more typically provided on a one-to-one basis such as infant massage, Video Interaction Guidance and parent-infant psychotherapy. Furthermore, these approaches are on the whole best characterized as being 'attachment' based, aiming for the better part to promote the type of early interactions between parent and baby that will result in him or her being 'securely attached'. The evidence regarding the benefits of such attachment is now substantive, as is the evidence about the long-term problems that can follow from an 'insecure' or 'disorganized' attachment (Fearon *et al.* 2010; Sroufe 2005; Steel and Siever 2010).

The chapters also build into a clear vision in terms of the way in which such groups can be developed and delivered across a range of settings (e.g. healthy baby clinics, children's centres and NHS perinatal mental health services) and contexts (e.g. UK, Europe and Africa).

This book also describes a number of ways in which practitioners can be supported to provide the alpha function through supervision and other methods such as the teaching of attunement. This **parallel process** of containment across the practitioner-parent-baby triad is now recognized to be an integral part of the effectiveness of early interventions, and may be particularly important for practitioners working not only to understand the lives of the participating parent-baby dyads, but to manage the dynamics of the group as well. It was the psychoanalyst Bion (1961) who identified the way in which the emotions of a group can prevent it from achieving its overall aim with the danger of defences such as 'flight or flight' and 'dependency' undermining its core activity, and the role of supervisors in helping the practitioners to identify and address this. And it was another psychoanalyst, Michael Balint, who recognized the importance not only of the group as a 'safe space', but also of the role of the supervisor in terms of enabling practitioners to think more deeply about the possible psychological basis of many physical problems, and the way in which such problems can be managed and contained.

This book is a cradle full of wonderful examples of working that will change your thinking about how best to support parents and babies during the perinatal period, and will be a joy to read for anyone who has a passion for infant mental health.

Jane Barlow
Oxford
October 2016

REFERENCES

Balint, M. (1957) The Doctor, His Patient and the Illness. London: Churchill Livingstone.

Bion, W.R. (1961) *Experiences in Groups, and Other Papers*. London: Tavistock.

Bion, W.R. (1962) 'A theory of thinking.' *International Journal of Psycho-Analysis 43*. Reprinted in W.R. Bion (1967) *Second Thoughts*. London: Karnac.

Fearon, R.P., Bakermans-Kranenburg, M.J., van Ijzendoorn, M.H., Lapsley, A.M. and Roisman, G.I. (2010) 'The significance of insecure attachment and disorganization in the development of children's externalizing behavior: a meta-analytic study.' *Child Development 81*, 435–456.

Fonagy, P. (2001) *Attachment Theory and Psychoanalysis*. New York: Other Press.

Kane, G.A., Wood, V.A. and Barlow, J. (2007) 'Parenting programmes: a systematic review and synthesis of qualitative research.' *Child: Care, Health and Development 33*, 6, 784–793.

Meins, E., Fernyhough, C., deRosnay, M., Arnott, B., Leekam, S.R. and Turner, M. (2012) 'Mind-mindedness as a multidimensional construct: appropriate and nonattuned mind-related comments independently predict infant–mother attachment in a socially diverse sample.' *Infancy 17*, 4, 393–415.

Meins, E., Fernyhough, C., Fradley, E. and Tuckey, M. (2001) 'Rethinking maternal sensitivity: mothers' comments on infants' mental processes predict security of attachment at 12 months.' *Journal of Child Psychology and Psychiatry 42*, 637–648.

Schore, A.N. (2001) 'Effects of a secure attachment relationship on right brain development, affect regulation, and infant mental health.' *Infant Mental Health Journal 22*, 7–66.

Sroufe, L.A. (2005) 'Attachment and development: a prospective, longitudinal study from birth to adulthood.' *Attachment & Human Development 7*, 4, 349–367.

Steele, H. and Siever, L. (2010) 'An attachment perspective on borderline personality disorder: advances in gene–environment considerations.' *Current Psychiatry Reports 12*, 1, 61–67.

Acknowledgements

The production of this book has benefitted from the help of many people, colleagues, family and friends, who have given their time generously to consult, advise and support me over the year of writing. Special thanks go to Rebecca Foster, whose diligence, patience and thoughtfulness have helped to turn what sometimes seemed like a mountain of words into coherent English. Thank you to the staff at Jessica Kingsley Publishers, to the many external readers, and to the Oxford Parent Infant Project, who gave me the opportunity to lead many groups of parents and babies.

Most of all I am grateful to all the mothers, fathers, babies and toddlers who shared parts of their life journey, their joys and difficulties, and who gave permission to use their stories in this book.

LIST OF EXTERNAL READERS

Robin Balbernie, Tessa Baradon, Jo Birbeck, Anne Burns, Paula Carr, Robin Celebi, Sulia Celebi, Anne Denny, Sue Einhorn, Polly Ferguson, Pam Fisher, Rebecca Foster, Margaret Gallop, Barbara Grossman, David Hadley, Sally Hogg, Anne Holmes, Helen Howes, Jessica James, Jenny Jarvis, Hazel Jordan, Hilary Kennedy, Pavlina Lascaratou, Sissy Lykou, Debi Maskell-Graham, Anthia Navridi, Mary Nolan, Cynthia Payman, Terry Payman, Ronnie Plagerson, Robyn Pound, Sasha Roseneil, Angela Smith, Margaret Smith, Bobby Taylor, Liz Todd, Jan Tomlinson, Sarah Tucker, Antonella Villari, Karen Walker, Linde Wotton and Hilary Wright.

Introduction

Monika Celebi

When I first conceived the idea for *Weaving the Cradle*, I thought that this image clearly conveys the work so many of us do on a daily basis, when we facilitate groups for parents, babies and toddlers. Each and every thread, on its own, can break easily, yet together we strengthen the social fabric, which holds and supports the parents, so they in turn can protect, soothe and look after their babies.

I decided early on to use the term 'baby' rather than 'infant'. This has proved to be rather controversial. 'Infant' is more academic, more likely to be taken seriously and to be picked up by the 'right' search engines. At the same time, though, it creates a distance. I am more likely to read about an infant in a textbook than coo over one.

The word 'baby' on the other hand evokes more immediate feeling responses, and feelings are at the heart of our work with parent-baby and toddler groups. The intention of this volume is to engage you, the reader, to think about the emotional impact of groups, on all participants: parents, babies in utero and outside, toddlers and facilitators. It aims to give voice to frontline professionals, to provide a flavour of the actual experience of leading groups for parents who are expecting, or recently had babies, and what it feels like to be in such a group.

The period before and after birth is an extremely important window of opportunity, a time of immense changes, which raises anxieties as well as hopes. Overwhelming evidence that 'it is crucial to intervene early to promote infant mental health and to reduce the risk of children's development being hampered by abuse, neglect or other early parent-child relationship difficulties' has now been accumulated (WAVE Trust with Department for Education 2013, p.2), hammering home the point that investment in the 1001 critical days from conception to the age of two years (Leadsom *et al.* 2014) both brings multiple returns to society economically as well as helping families to avoid hardship and heartache.

The ultimate purpose of all groups in the perinatal period is to help parents to become more attuned, sensitive, mind-minded and empathic towards their babies and toddlers. This is especially important when the parents themselves have not had this experience in their own lives. We aim to reduce the transmission of trans-generational patterns of abuse, neglect, anxiety and depression. We do this by creating positive environments where genuine interest and empathy can grow. Clinical experience shows repeatedly how attuned, contingent and appropriate interventions can significantly improve the outcomes for the families and their babies and toddlers.

Weaving the Cradle sets out to demonstrate central themes of groups, whether they take place before or after birth. In the antenatal period they have the potential to foster parents' thinking about their babies early on and positively impact on the representation of their baby. They can help parents regulate their emotions and prepare for the transition to parenthood. After the birth, groups of parents and babies/toddlers together with their facilitators can generate a matrix (Bion 2014), a web of relationships, where all are equal participants, communicating verbally as well as non-verbally, harnessing the 'seeking systems' of the babies and toddlers and enhancing the 'care systems' in the parents (Panksepp and Biven 2007).

This book is the collaborative effort of 31 pioneering professionals in the field of groups for parents, babies and toddlers. It describes best practice as well as challenges. Whilst most examples are from the UK, chapters describing projects in Asia and Africa highlight how similar and how massive the needs of mothers, fathers and babies are there. Despite the cultural, political and socioeconomic differences, the principles underlying group work with parents and babies and toddlers are the same everywhere.

Each practitioner/author brings his or her own unique perspective, which contributes to the richness of this field. *Weaving the Cradle* hopes to illuminate the thinking and guiding principles behind their work and to describe the variety of methods and their practical applications in different settings, at different stages of the perinatal period, from antenatal groups to groups in the first six months, the first year and the second year of a baby's life.

The book is divided into five sections. Section I describes groups for parents and babies and toddlers, run in community and health settings in the UK and in Greece, including a midwifery-led project. Section II focuses on groups that use video to enhance parental attunement. Section III gives examples of groups where parents had a psychiatric/psychotherapeutic referral, or are in the family courts, as a result of safeguarding concerns. Section IV describes antenatal and postnatal psycho-educational programmes in the UK and abroad. Section V gives a taste of reflective practice to support those who are leading the groups for parents, babies and toddlers.

Weaving the Cradle could not have been written without the generous permission of parents, who shared their stories and their gorgeous babies with us. Unless stated otherwise, details have been changed, creating composites to keep the spirit, and to protect our parents' identity to avoid all recognition. We respect their privacy and the trust they have given us when they allowed us this intimate access at such a critical time in their lives. The authors are deeply grateful and humbled by parents' and babies' resilience, perseverance and courage often in the face of hardship and difficulties.

Groups in the perinatal period can provide a haven of support, a time to slow down, to become more relaxed, less anxious and fully present with the experience of becoming a parent and being thoughtful of their baby/toddler. This includes allowing, tolerating and naming the challenges, yet the focus is building on existing strengths.

Cradles from all cultures have in common that they are containing, flexible, strong, safe and soothing. Group interventions that are mindful, reflective and attuned can have such an impact. Clinical work demonstrates repeatedly how much parents and babies/toddlers benefit from being in an accepting, genuinely curious and friendly containing group environment with a thoughtful group facilitator. The methods vary. What counts is mindfulness, being non-judgemental towards the parents and themselves as facilitators, plus an understanding that groups have the potential to amplify the experiences of all.

Frontline workers who are weaving these cradles see on a daily basis that parent-baby and toddler groups are a way that offers an alternative when the internal, familial and social fabric that families occupy has been damaged. They often provide families with significant positive experiences of support and care. This helps them and their babies and toddlers to thrive. This book is a celebration of what has been achieved and a recognition of how much more we still need to do.

REFERENCES

Bion, W.R. (2014) *Experiences in Groups, and Other Papers*. London: Routledge.

Leadsom, A., Field, F., Burstow, P. and Lucas, C. (2014) *The 1001 Critical Days: The Importance of the Conception to Age Two Period*. Available at: http://www. andrealeadsom.com/downloads/1001cdmanifesto.pdf (Accessed: 1 December 2016).

Panksepp, J. and Biven, L. (2007) *The Archaeology of Mind: Neuroevolutionary Origins of Human Emotions*. New York: W.W. Norton.

WAVE Trust in collaboration with Department for Education (2013) *Conception to Age 2 – The Age of Opportunity. Addendum to the Government's Vision for the Foundation Years: 'Supporting Families in the Foundation Years'*. Available at: http:// www.wavetrust.org/our-work/publications/reports/conception-age-2-age-opportunity (Accessed: 1 December 2016).

SUPPORTING EARLY ATTACHMENT IN THE COMMUNITY

CHAPTER 1

Weaving the Cradle

Therapeutic Touch Groups – A Portal to Engage
Parents and Support Sensitive Caregiving

Monika Celebi, Camille Kalaja and Bobby Taylor

In this chapter we describe how we facilitate Therapeutic Touch groups to support the development of attuned and sensitive responsiveness, which underlies secure attachment. Examples from groups at a children's centre, a military base, and an NHS health centre aim to bring the work to life.

ABOUT US

Bobby and Monika are parent infant psychotherapists and Camille Kalaja is a maternity outreach worker. We also trained in baby massage and embodied **mentalization** (using one's visceral response to intuit another's needs and feelings).

Over 800 parents and their babies have attended our groups in the last ten years in children's centres and one health centre, in and around Oxford. With few exceptions most of the parents were mothers.

THEORETICAL BACKGROUND

We combine a reflective stance on conscious and unconscious processes of communication with the action-based structure of baby massage. The overall aim is to create a calm and connect system (de Zulueta 2006; Moberg 2011), which activates the **mammalian vagus**. This is the part of the nervous system, involved in care-taking (de Zulueta 2016), which helps parents to regulate themselves and their young to contain and soothe the primitive anxieties that babies can arouse (Baradon *et al.* 2015). Relaxed parents can start observing and thinking of what may be going on in baby's mind and body and start naming feelings. Often, after stroking and massaging, mothers will be less defensive and start talking about hopes, worries and fears.

They also become more open to learning additional ways of interacting with their baby other than 'just' feeding and cleaning. Women can then allow themselves to be vulnerable and feel free to ask the questions that matter to them (de Zulueta 2016). They become more receptive to useful information, providing ideal opportunities for psycho-education, such as how to help babies to sleep without reverting to 'controlled crying'.

Physical touch evokes profound feelings in all of us, it can be soothing or stimulating, it can be abusive or intrusive, and it can conjure up unconscious good or painful memories (Celebi 2013; Van der Kolk 2015). A premature baby may have very sensitive feet as a result of medical procedures and not enjoy having their feet touched. We have to be careful in making assumptions. Early experiences of touch, however, do provide the blueprint for the quality of contact babies expect from their environment.

SENSITIVE TOUCH

Even though groups are advertised in various ways, for instance as baby massage and baby chatting, their purpose is to teach not massage but sensitive touch, whereby parents are asked to follow their baby's cues, rather than a 'correct' massage routine. An anxious mother may need help to be more intentional and reassuring. A parent who consistently misreads their baby's cues will be encouraged to sit back, watch and be curious, rather than 'do' (Underdown, Norwood and Barlow 2013). Encouraging parents to wonder what each baby likes, moment by moment, is at the heart of Therapeutic Touch groups.

A COMFORTABLE ENVIRONMENT

A private, clean, soft and friendly environment is crucial. As mothers have recently given birth, their bodies maybe traumatized and need help to sit comfortably in a variety of ways; we are usually on the floor in a circle, with the babies in the middle. Cushions can be important to alleviate discomfort, which creates stress. Only then will mothers be free to become more attentive and friendly to their babies.

A NON-THREATENING ACTIVITY

Therapeutic Touch groups have been especially effective in engaging hard to reach parents to take part in an activity such as baby massage (which parents consider to be helpful also with sleeping, digesting and soothing and concrete tasks they are already doing all the time around the clock). When they follow the invitation to join the group, they have a reason to leave the house with baby (which can be difficult, especially if a mother is depressed) and become part of a welcoming environment with other parents who are at a similar stage of parenting.

ACTIVITIES TO DECREASE STRESS

The group includes simple and repetitive activities, such as stroking, gentle massage routines, singing familiar nursery rhymes and rocking the babies, as well as wondering about baby's feelings. Repetitive movements impact on the nervous system of *all* the group participants and elicit a collective relaxation response, which reduces the heart rate, blood pressure and muscular tension, as well as increasing levels of oxytocin and endorphin (Field 2002).

CREATING A SENSE OF TOGETHERNESS
– SINGING A LULLABY

At the end of each session parents wrap their babies in a blanket, holding them closely whilst singing a lullaby and rocking. As facilitators, we do the same with our massage dolls. This can be a magical moment of togetherness. Even self-conscious mothers may still be able to join in by humming along. Seeing others hugging their babies combined with the repetitive motions impacts directly on a parent's physical and emotional relationship with their baby.

MONIKA'S GROUP AT A CHILDREN'S CENTRE

Lorna had been abused and neglected as a child. Aged 14, she ran away and lived on an abandoned building site. She had her first baby when she was 16, whom she said was 'like a devil' when she cried. This daughter was removed into foster care. Five years later, Lorna gave birth a second time. Her baby was two months premature and small. The professional system was concerned and so the baby was put on a Child Protection Plan and they were referred to the Therapeutic Touch group.

Initially Lorna just sat with us, while her baby slept in the pram. Eventually, after several weeks attending in this way, she took her baby out of the pram; first just holding her, then gradually she started playing with her hand and toes, stroking them. When we sang the lullaby she held her baby and gently swayed with the rhythm of the song. She, and the 'baby in her', needed this soothing motion, and experience, as much as her real baby. In her feedback Lorna said later, 'When we sang the lullaby, I felt we were all together, helping each other, to comfort the babies.'

Lorna attended the group for six months. In the end she became the spokesperson for the group who explained to new mothers: 'Here we do what the babies like, you can just relax and your baby will like it.'

TICKLING, NURSERY RHYMES AND PARENTAL AMBIVALENCE

Tickling is often a disputed subject. Initially parents may say their babies like it, because they laugh. This may, however, be a nervous response, which is reflexive and anxious, as excitement that easily tips into fear builds up (Phillips 1993). Lots of nursery rhymes encourage tickling, but I tend to question if babies really like it, as I have not yet met a parent who in discussions will share positive memories about it. Reasons for tickling are complex.

Nursery rhymes in general can express a certain amount of cruelty or ambivalence, and are a good starting point to discuss some of the complicated feelings parents may have towards their babies. For instance, 'Rock-a-Bye-Baby' describes how the wind rocks the cradle, but 'when the bough breaks, the cradle will fall', which is a potentially deadly turn of events.

To break the cycle of abuse and harshness towards babies, I found it helpful to allow the expression of ambivalence many parents feel towards their babies, but also contain and combine it with guidance towards sensitive touch.

SUPPORTING REGULATION AND CONTAINMENT

Dirshana's pregnancy had been full of health complications and the birth was 'managed'. She believed others understood her baby Hira better than she did. She struggled to comfort her and said Hira always screamed herself to sleep, while she had to rock her strongly. In the group this looked like she was shaking her and it was extremely stressful to watch.

Once when this happened I approached her, stood very close and started talking to both mother and the upset baby, in **parentese** (with high-pitched, elongated vowels), saying, 'Oh, I can see; this is difficult for you and for your mummy.' I was looking for a meeting place with the crying baby, whose panic and distress were so contagious, whilst acknowledging the mother's discomfort at being seen not to cope.

Soothing voice

Eventually we managed to calm down together. My notes after this session read:

> I was talking to all the parents and the babies, as well as the babies within the parents, when I adjusted my body, position, and voice. It seems to be the way I speak, the melody, rather than the meaning of the words, which had most impact.

PRIMARY MATERNAL PREOCCUPATION

The ideal window of opportunity for the Therapeutic Touch groups is when the babies are three to six months old, and totally focused on the mother or primary attachment figure, and vice versa, benefitting from 'primary maternal preoccupation' (Winnicott 2013), which coincides with a period of growth spurts and strengthening of neural pathways (Gerhardt 2014) in the baby.

CAMILLE'S GROUP AT A HEALTH CENTRE

I am employed by the local children's centre, which has for the last eight years collaborated with a nursery nurse, who is attached to the local health visiting team. This joined-up working allows us to get to know all new parents in the neighbourhood, and to use the room in the local health centre, where the baby clinic, familiar to the parents, is held. The chairs are moved alongside the walls, and rugs and duvets are placed in the centre of the room. The groups run for five weeks each and participants can attend several blocks.

My co-worker, a nursery nurse, and I alternate the leading of the Therapeutic Touch sessions, so the other can be present and observe, as a key part of our work, as is the modelling of interactions and being in a supportive role for the participants.

A PRECIOUS MOMENT

Mother Emily was anxious 'to do well'. She had found the group stressful to begin with. During the third session, Connie, her three-month-old, seemed to enjoy the massage and spent some time looking at her surroundings. Emily was worried that Connie did not look at her as much as other babies looked at their own mothers.

Towards the end of the session, encouraged by our suggestions, Emily put her hands gently around her baby's face, stroking her whilst smiling. Suddenly Connie vocalized her contentment by producing some gorgeous sounds of satisfaction. The baby sustained eye contact with her mother and continued expressing herself. Emily had a rush of emotions; she blushed and shed tears of joy, and quietly started laughing and crying all at the same time.

I felt privileged to observe that brief moment. I approached Emily towards the end of the session and shared with her that I had noticed their exquisite moment of contact. I wondered with her what her baby might have wanted to express. Mother agreed that it was a precious interaction. I was keen to hear mother Emily's thoughts on what baby Connie may have been saying, if she had words. Then I offered my own interpretation, and talking for the baby I said, 'Mummy, I love when you massage me so gently, especially my face. It relaxes me and when I turn around I see you here looking over me lovingly.'

REFLECTION

This gentle intervention allowed the mother to appreciate and recognize even more the powerful moment she had shared with her baby as important and real. It was what Emily had longed for. By witnessing and commenting on this very special connection indirectly, via baby Connie, Camille had supported mother's fledgling self-esteem in her role as a parent. This helped to validate mother and her baby's feelings and their connection, strengthening the basis for their long-term relationship.

BOBBY'S GROUP – ON A MILITARY BASE

The following is an example of a father's unexpected presence in a group. This weekly group was number four out of a block of six sessions.

It was made up of five mothers and their babies, aged between three and five months. Carol had unexpectedly brought her husband Jim, as she wanted him to 'see what it was like', and how hard it was to look after their baby Becky, a common theme in this group.

Martha's husband was stationed abroad. When at home, he was not 'in tune' with either mother or baby, Tom. Martha was isolated from her family of origin, who only gave conditional critical support via Skype, focusing on Tom's bodily state rather than his emotional needs. She experienced Tom as demanding, but also as fragile and difficult to understand.

Jenny, a soldier, was doubly isolated, as there were not many soldier mothers and the base itself was detached from the civilian local neighbourhood. Her husband, not a soldier, worked away from home for long periods and she felt 'just like a single mum'. Prior to the birth she had lost a beloved sister, whom she missed badly. She felt unable to breastfeed and wanted her baby, Joan, to be 'independent', that is, to be propped up so she could hold the bottle herself, rather than being held snuggly for feeding. Jenny said the days were long and she felt very lonely. Baby Joan did not smile much.

Carol instructed Jim, 'You can hold her, and I'll have a break.' Jim looked uneasy, but did what he was told. I offered Carol a massage doll, to practise the strokes. She laughed, 'So much easier than a real baby.' The group then talked about the differences between the baby dolls and the real babies, who are lively, interactive, sometimes delicious and yummy, and sometimes very demanding and hard work.

Carol kept checking over at her husband, who was sitting, leaning his back on the wall and positioning Becky upright on his lap. I invited the group to ask their babies if they wanted to be massaged. Jim decided that Becky did not want to join in, much to Carol's annoyance as, 'she always loves it,' but he said, 'Becky is fine, she's just concentrating on something else,' which the group understood to mean she was trying to do a poo. At this point Becky went very red in the face and emitted an amazingly loud sound of evacuation of the bowel! The tone of the group shifted instantly to one of laughter.

Carol then talked with nervous giggles about how worried she had been about her daughter's supposed constipation problem – with inconsistent advice from professionals, her mother and friends.

Initially Martha and Jenny had positioned their babies on the floor facing away from them, and the mothers leant back and 'rested', while the babies attempted in vain to engage with them. I suggested we sing a familiar nursery rhyme, while starting to massage our babies' legs. Martha and Jenny leant forward to stroke their babies, whilst Becky and her father sat watching us. She, by now, was clearly having a very successful emptying-the-bowel moment, much to the amusement of the room and the pride of her parents! Together they cleaned up as we continued the massage routine singing and stroking.

As the atmosphere in the room relaxed, the mothers shifted their attention to their own babies. Martha turned baby Tom round, who was now facing her, much to his obvious delight. Baby Joan, who had been lying next to the very active cleaning-up process, increased her whole body movements and vocalizations. Finally, mother Jenny reached down and locking her fingers into Joan's little hand, smiled at her, and said, 'Are you trying to talk to me?'

REFLECTION

The arrival in this session of Jim, the new group member, meant that all had to re-establish the boundaries created over the first three weeks. This provided a challenge in terms of the **containment** and holding of the group. Lack of fathers both in the mothers' histories and in their present circumstances was a common theme, however, so Jim's arrival into the group seemed pivotal. He was able to play his part by managing baby Becky and her mother's anxieties and allow the voicing of mixed feelings. Perhaps he also helped contain the other mothers in order for them in turn to become more sensitive to their babies.

It seemed as though the father, noticing that his daughter did not want to engage in the massage process, by quite literally holding and containing her, helped the other parents to finally see their own babies' needs in that very moment.

LAYLA'S FEEDBACK

I wanted to become a mum, but the birth was traumatic, and I was so badly injured I had to live with my in-laws, as my parents are abroad. I was smiling, pretending to be happy, when I was in agony, and too weak to hold my baby.

She got used to the bottle, even though I had lots of milk. I was very sad about this, felt guilty and ended up expressing milk for nine months. In hindsight I can say I was depressed. When you invited me to come to the baby massage group I started my journey of recovery. You made me feel special, and that I mattered, I felt so warm and welcome.

I used to think constantly: what is wrong with me? and I was too shy to talk to someone about what I was going through. In the group you did not have to talk. It was healing like taking antibiotics. No one criticized me. I felt that I was accepted as I am. I remember when I first came I touched my son's foot. I held it in my hand and I kissed it, and I thought that even though he was three months already, I was seeing this foot for the very first time.

TO CONCLUDE

In this chapter we have tried to give a feel for how three practitioners working in different settings use both similar and different ways of reaching out and engaging with parents and babies, yet all have created an environment where parents could lower their defences and be with their babies in attuned and sensitive ways, whatever that might be at that time. Not all parents are able to take advantage and attend, even if the groups are available, because they may feel too vulnerable. If parents are too fragile to attend, offering one-to-one sessions can be an alternative.

Ultimately Therapeutic Touch groups aim to make space for mutual delight and pleasure. When parents can shift from being anxious to feeling accepted and safe, they can relate with more kindness to themselves, and to their babies. This can strengthen babies' neural pathways underlying secure attachment, and is conducive to developing loving relationships. The impact of the quality of early parenting on later life is well established (Gerhardt 2014). This is why it is so important to support parents early on to hold and handle their babies with sensitivity. It would be ideal if all parents had access to such groups in their local area.

REFERENCES

Baradon, T., with Broughton, C., Gibbs, I., James, J., Joyce, A. and Woodhead, J. of the Parent-Infant Project at the Anna Freud Centre (2015) *The Practice of Psychoanalytic Parent-Infant Psychotherapy: Claiming the Baby*. New York: Taylor & Francis.

Celebi, M. (2013) 'Helping to reduce parental anxiety in the perinatal period.' *Journal of Health Visiting 1*, 8, 438–442.

de Zulueta, F. (2006) *From Pain to Violence: The Traumatic Roots of Destructiveness*. 2nd edn. Chichester: John Wiley & Sons.

de Zulueta, F. (2016) Personal communication. 13 July.

Field, T. (2002) 'Infants' need for touch.' *Human Development 45*, 2, 100–103.

Gerhardt, S. (2014) *Why Love Matters: How Affection Shapes a Baby's Brain*. 2nd edn. London: Routledge.

Moberg, K.U. (2011) *The Oxytocin Factor: Tapping the Hormone of Calm, Love, and Healing*. London: Pinter & Martin.

Phillips, A. (1993) *On Kissing, Tickling and Being Bored: Psychoanalytic Essays on the Unexamined Life*. London: Faber and Faber.

Underdown, A., Norwood, R. and Barlow, J. (2013) 'A realist evaluation of the processes and outcomes of infant massage programs.' *Infant Mental Health Journal 34*, 6, 483–495.

Van der Kolk, B.A. (2015) *The Body Keeps the Score: Brain, Mind, and Body in the Healing of Trauma*. New York: Penguin Books.

Winnicott, D.W. (ed.) (2013) *Collected Papers: Through Paediatrics to Psychoanalysis*. London: Routledge.

CHAPTER 2

Health Care Baby Clinics

Opportunities for Developing Emotionally Rewarding
Group Experiences between Parents and Babies

Jessica James

SUMMARY

In this chapter, I describe how local and universal health care baby clinics can be developed into group settings to strengthen parent and baby relationships. Drawing upon experiences from previous projects, I will illustrate what can happen between babies, parents and staff members, including myself as facilitator, in the inter-connected spaces built around the mats 'weaving the cradle' on the baby clinic floor. I also reflect on the outcomes and implications of this work.

BACKGROUND

I have become increasingly interested in how a collection of families coming to have their babies weighed in a health care clinic could become an emotionally rewarding, baby friendly, mini-community. My idea is that such ordinary settings are opportunities for therapeutic experiences, which offer new possibilities for parent and baby relating and a sense of belonging with others. Such an attachment-focused approach can also facilitate the practice of health care staff teams through more natural observations of parent and baby relating than a more traditional, formal one. This can inform their professional thinking and subsequent interventions, both inside and outside the baby clinic.

I am a group analyst specializing in parent infant psychotherapy and have been involved in a number of projects where we have remodelled clinics to create a more playful and interactive group culture alongside the provision of routine health care and advice (James 2016; Sleed *et al.* 2013).

LINKING UP PHYSICAL AND EMOTIONAL HEALTH

Baby clinics are a universal service providing an important source of support for families in the UK. They are valued and well attended, especially by the most socially disadvantaged hard to reach families who appreciate the concrete reassurance and baby care advice offered in these local, drop-in settings (Callan 2008). However, physical wellbeing tends to be given priority over emotional wellbeing and visits are not always the experience they could be. The focus is upon checking babies and talking to parents, as efficiently as possible in busy, goal-driven environments within a waiting-room atmosphere.

The clinics' aims are to monitor and support babies' healthy development, but the babies themselves are frequently talked *about* rather than *with*, and are not related to as persons in their own right. This is despite what we know about mothers and babies in the first year of life: that bodies and minds are not yet partitioned (Kraemer 2016), but inextricably linked, and that this is a critical period for brain development, which depends upon the emotional experiences received from the very beginning of life (Perry 2004).

OPPORTUNITIES FOR MAKING CONNECTIONS

Baby clinics offer ideal environments for encouraging attuned relating with babies *there and then*, to *being* rather than *doing*. A group culture can be fostered with a slow pace that has forms of communicating conducive to both babies and their parents, some of whom have only just given birth. Parents overwhelmed by stresses and practical difficulties can gain mutual support and a refocus upon what the majority want most of all: the best for their babies. The non-stigmatizing concrete care becomes a *weigh* in (*way* in) to a supportive experience for at risk and disadvantaged families who are often extremely difficult to engage in children's centre groups or psychological services. It provides the opportunity to integrate physical and mental infant health 'now, not later', through weighing babies in an ordinary health care baby clinic setting. It becomes possible to reach the most vulnerable parents and babies and provide a therapeutic baby-centred group environment alongside concrete practical care.

AIMS AND DESCRIPTION OF THE PROJECT

The pilot project 'Now, Not Later: Strengthening Parent and Infant Relationships in a Universal Baby Clinic' was funded by the Winnicott Trust in 2013 and ran for a year at a baby clinic in a deprived inner city area.

THE AIMS

- To bring babies' emotional development more to the forefront.

- To help parents get more out of their experience at the clinic, through staff encouraging and modelling playful interactions and ways of responding sensitively to babies.

- To make the baby clinic a place where issues can be raised that impact on the parent's mood, such as if there are difficulties within the family or postnatal depression, and responses discussed.

PREPARING FOR THE PROJECT

I had helped set up the project and worked as a clinician on the mat each week, along with a volunteer play worker. We had meetings with the health visiting team before, during and after the project to discuss our aims, to plan and think about our work together. Researchers planned an innovative evaluation, which included filming from a bird's-eye view, to show the flow of interactions between staff, parents and babies, before and after the clinic was remodelled.

WHAT WAS THE BABY CLINIC LIKE BEFORE
AND AFTER REMODELLING?

The following descriptions are mine, giving as objective account as possible, taken from five-minute film clips of the clinic, first when run traditionally and then once the remodelled project had run for a year.

Before and after remodelling

Before: parents sit on adult sized chairs placed around the edge of a large room, with small mats in the middle and a slide. Smaller babies are on knees; older ones are at their parents' feet, either sitting, walking around or on the slide. Babies are looking in different directions from their parents and there is a sense of everyone alone waiting for something to happen. After: parents, staff and babies are seated low down within the room's centre, mostly on big mats or on small chairs at the edge of the mats. A few parents are on high chairs with small babies on their knees.

Before: conversations are between the staff members and parents, sitting next to each other. A one-year-old is staggering around, dripping milk from his bottle, and a staff member mops it up whilst his mother is looking at her mobile phone. After: there is a sense of activity and movement, with babies joining in conversations and people engaging with each other. Rattles and toys are being used by adults, trying to interest young babies, and older babies are picking toys up, exploring them with their hands and mouths. Newcomers are welcomed, and babies are greeted alongside parents.

Before: a few toddlers show interest in each other and congregate briefly. A staff member crouches down next to a toddler with a box of toys but, when she leaves, he loses interest in the toys and toddles off.

After: some babies are sitting on the mat, interacting together with their bodies and limbs moving responsively whilst their parents talk to each other. I try to help a mother and baby enjoy a rattle, pointing out that he is responding with his whole body and helping her take the rattle to him in a way he can manage.

Before: a staff member and mother are talking, but the mother is jumping up every so often to help her toddler on the slide. She looks as though she is finding it difficult to concentrate on the adult discussion. After: a staff member sits down next to a mother and father, who are looking towards their toddler and seem engaged in the conversations.

Before: the sounds are predominately loud banging and screeching that is often sudden. After: the sounds are lower, buzzy and mostly with a constant hum.

An analysis of my descriptions of the 'before' and 'after' film clips
In this Section I am also taking into account the responses of different professional audiences who have seen them.

Both clips have similar numbers of people in the clinics, but 'before', the room seems emptier, with parents and babies dispersed and in separate islands. There is a sense that everyone is up and vertical, rather than across, as in 'after', where more are at a similar level on the mat.

In 'before', babies are mostly alone, sometimes searching as if to say, 'Is anyone out there?', showing a desire for relating and playing with toys, but losing those moments without adults supporting them. In 'after' there is a greater sense of coherence with parents and babies more engaged, communicating and interacting non-verbally. Some are sitting alone, but appear stimulated by the activities in the room, whereas 'before' parents and babies were staring into space, looking tense or using mobiles.

'Before' is an environment where families are being shut up and cleared up (as in the bottle spillage), whilst 'after' there is greater interest in making contact and an openness to things being difficult, such as sometimes trying and failing to play.

In 'before' there are more unsettled babies, with parents exposed and frustrated within a large empty space, whilst in 'after', nearly everyone seems involved within a rhythmic flow.

EXPERIENCES OF THE PARTICIPANTS – FOUR VOICES

In this section I express the different experiences of a parent, her baby, my colleague and me, as I believe they might be spoken in our own voices. My hope is to help the reader enter into the individual perspectives and understand how a group setting can be interactive and emotionally supportive. Speaking from the baby's perspective is unusual and reinforces one of the project's main aims: to bring babies' emotional development to the forefront.

Baby Asma

I come often and my mum brings me. We go and sit on a soft floor, there are toys and lots of other people at the same level as me. It's different from home, where most of the time I am on a bed with the television on and my mum is busy.

When I first came here my mum didn't help me with the strange place and people. She felt stiff and awkward and then suddenly I was left alone in the middle of the room, I didn't know where she was; it was overwhelming with all the rattles and strange noises. When my mum came back she pushed some rattles close to my face and they scared me, then suddenly she put another one there and before I had time to look at it, she took it away.

After a while I got used to it. I liked the slow feeling and the people who looked at me and who started to make noises like mine. I tried out sitting and grabbing things, and putting them in my mouth. I saw babies a bit like me and sometimes we looked at each other and wobbled in similar ways as we learnt to sit up by ourselves.

My mum and I started to sit closer together, she laughed with other mothers and I liked that noise and the feeling it gave me. She began to play with me at home like we do in the clinic. She seemed pleased with me and showed the lady what I have learnt to do. As I come here again and again, I learn that people here know me. When we go I wave my arms and legs, and people wave with me; sometimes I notice when other babies go and my mum and I wave with them as well.

Baby Asma's mother

I go to the clinic to get my baby weighed, to get injections and advice. I don't have far to go and I can go whenever I like and it's good to be told my baby is healthy. But it isn't like a usual clinic waiting room and we are asked to go with our babies onto the mats and the health visitor comes and talks there.

At first I felt awkward as I wasn't sure what to do and wanted not to be noticed and to get out as quickly as possible. I felt lonely, as my English isn't good. There were toys but my baby is too young to play and didn't seem interested anyway. The health visitor seemed to be telling me things and I didn't really understand what she wanted.

I can come and go as I like, but now I see that my baby likes it I stay longer. The women are helpful, they say hello to my baby and help her play. They remember us, so do other mothers, and I get ideas like I didn't know that I could talk with my baby, with noises and funny faces. One time she cried and I felt like leaving, but they helped calm her down. Sometimes I see other babies crying and getting help too. I'm surprised to see other parents don't always know what their babies want and I've noticed some parents getting upset, and I feel for them. It was good to tell the health visitor about my older child left behind in my country, and I felt she understood. Now my baby is one of the bigger ones and I look at the younger ones and remember what it was like, sometimes I enjoy playing with them too.

The facilitator (known as parent infant specialist)

On any given clinic day I don't know who is coming, but I hope baby Asma and her mum will return. It was worrying to see how disengaged they are from each other, how mother handles her abruptly and looks so sad. She seemed to find my attempts to help them play intrusive and it resulted in even more abrupt contact. She didn't seem to understand the health visitor's attempts either, looking away and playing with a rattle herself. We talked about our concerns after the clinic.

Who shall I go to talk with? Where shall I focus? There's a baby staring into space while her mother is chatting animatedly. I'll go and see if I can talk with them. I said to baby, 'Mummy has got lots to say, let's see if you can join in too.' I'm bringing a rattle and, along with using my face and voice, I place myself alongside baby's mother. 'Oh yes, it's nice to talk. Mummy is having a chat and you're joining in, moving with your whole body.' To mum, 'She seems interested in your conversation.' To another baby, who crawls over, 'Are you joining in too?' I make arm movements with the babies and look to their mothers' faces to share their babies' fascination in each other.

I am pleased to notice baby Asma and her mother arrive, but they have sat down apart. I must be cautious not to rush in and overwhelm them. I look around the room again and engage with others, possibly as a way of regulating my anxiety. I see an established mother go over to baby Asma and offer a rattle in a way that makes it easy for her to take. This mother smiles with baby Asma's mother and asks them something. I use this as an opportunity to join in and affirm the other mother's interest. I try to help baby Asma with the rattle and she responds animatedly and then, a little later, calls me back with little noises when I look away, which relieves me. I'm glad the health visitor has arranged an interpreter to find out what is going on.

The health visitor (based on conversations with my colleagues)

I wasn't sure why we had to change how the clinic is run. I had feedback that the parents liked the clinic, as it is. I didn't think they would want to spend time here playing with their babies; most of them seem to be in a hurry and I don't think we should impose play upon parents who are shy or find it culturally alien. I wondered how it would work having discussions on the mat; I'm not sure that my back is up to it. How about confidentiality, or if a parent got upset in that situation? I'm also not sure about the role of the parent infant specialist and how we will work together.

I've been surprised by how many parents come to the mat. It's amazing how the babies enjoy themselves and even the smallest ones sometimes come to kick and play amongst others. A three-year-old who I'd always seen clinging to her mother was going up and down on the slide with the play assistant's support and her mother looks happier than I've seen her before. I see what is going on better this way, I think parents put up a guard when they speak to someone but, when no one is actually talking to them, they interact more naturally, so we can observe and discuss this. I'm not sure the after-clinic meetings are necessary. I have my records to do and can't see the point in talking about difficulties when there is little that can be done.

I was worried about Asma and her mother, I tried to tell her about play but she couldn't take it in. She picked up Asma in such a rough way that other staff raised concerns too. It was useful to encourage them to come to the clinic, to gradually let them build up confidence and learn from others. I don't think she would have taken up a referral to the children's centre. We started to see Asma enjoy playing and I noticed her mother interacting more responsively. Sometimes I feel frustrated when we can't follow through the impact of our advice but, this way, with targeted families, we can work in more depth.

REFLECTIONS ON THE GROUP PROCESSES

I took the lead, as a magnet on the mat, in developing the culture, which aimed to foster a sense of group identity, thus adding another dimension to the traditional remit of the baby clinic. Professional collaboration was crucial as was being prepared to learn from each other in embracing the aims of the remodelled clinic. At times, we had to change the ways we worked. For instance, the health visiting team often needed to talk with families on the mat and, when engaging directly with the babies, join the playful atmosphere. I needed to be careful not to interfere with the running of the clinic, nor over-pathologize (focus on what was not going well) in my observations of parent-infant relating. When a group functioned well everyone contributed, including the babies. There was less emphasis on professional authority, and more inter-connectedness, all on a level on the mat.

Because everyone potentially sees and hears all the interactions, they impact on both the individuals concerned and the group culture as a whole. Enquiring faces, eyes lighting up or an attuned movement towards a baby can be a meaningful experience for everyone, even if the words are not actually heard or understood in the busy clinic.

I tended to ask straightforward questions to encourage exchanges between the parents and, over time, longer-standing parents became able to initiate similar conversations too. Throughout, babies were included as we engaged with them directly and encouraged them to join in. This became a model for parents, allowing them to see their babies as social, perhaps more capable and resilient than before (Bradley, Selby and Urwin 2012). For some babies this involved relational encounters that were quite different from before, and these kinds of experiences, although apparently small, can mean a lot (Berg 2012). I aimed to reinforce them, by commenting positively and by grabbing such moments, in recognition that parents and babies will not necessarily be there the following week.

EVALUATION

Feedback from parents, gathered through questionnaire-led interviews, was almost entirely positive. A mother of a nine-week-old baby said: 'Good for him; good stimulation to interact with things. He was following her; seeing her gestures. I felt happy 'cause he develops.'

Before the project, when asked about how their babies found the clinic, a number said they were too young to notice or play and others said their babies were bored. None said this when talking about the remodelled clinic. Some parents especially appreciated the social contact, such as this mother with a seven-month-old baby: 'It's nice and enjoyable. People talk about their experiences, especially with smaller babies when they might be depressed.'

Feedback from the health visiting team was less certain. Many valued the remodelled clinic, recognizing that having a specialist on the mat helped parents and babies to interact and enjoy the toys. One health visitor said, 'People felt that maybe parents might not want to come, but actually they enjoy coming and even stay a little longer.' Another said, 'It allows you to think more about how the children are interacting with their parents. Previously we would be more focused on maternal mood.' Other health visitors found the model an imposition and seemed happier returning to traditional ways at the end of the project. One said, 'It is not my job to sit on the floor and interact with the babies. I don't particularly want to take this responsibility.'

WHAT WE LEARNED

Many of the project's aims were met, such as to bring babies' emotional development more to the forefront and to encourage playful interactions with babies. It became clear that it is emotionally demanding to engage with babies as little persons with all their primitive needs, in combination with the pressures of the health visiting role.

The collaboration between disciplines within the clinic space and talking together with families to address issues that impacted upon the parents' mood was less successful. A year is probably not long enough to build sufficiently trusting working relationships for this to happen. There was some evidence that parents' mood was helped indirectly through the changed atmosphere in the clinic.

FUTURE PLANS

It is unrealistic to have parent infant psychotherapists in every baby clinic and it is anticipated that more sustainable culture change could be achieved if health visiting staff were supported to expand the role

of clinics themselves. Future projects involve lead health visitors, in particular perinatal and infant mental health specialists (NHS 2016), working jointly with parent infant psychotherapists to offer training and reflective sessions. It is hoped this will enable baby clinic teams to reconfigure and develop their clinics themselves, in relation to local need and with their own in-house 'mat facilitators'. Further research will determine the effectiveness and form the basis for conversations on the creative 'weaving the cradle' group possibilities within ordinary baby clinics, for enhanced infant mental health.

REFERENCES

Berg, A. (2012) 'When a little means a lot.' *The Signal: Newsletter of the World Association of Infant Mental Health 20*, 2, 1–5.
Bradley, B.S., Selby, J. and Urwin, C. (2012) 'Group Life in Babies: Opening Up Perceptions and Possibilities.' In C. Urwin and J. Sternberg (eds) *Infant Observation and Research: Emotional Processes in Everyday Lives*. London: Routledge.
Callan, S. (2008) *The Next Generation: A Policy Report from the Early Years Commission*. The Centre for Social Justice. Available at: http://www.centreforsocialjustice. org.uk/core/wp-content/uploads/2016/08/TheNextGenerationReportFINAL. pdf (Accessed: 1 December 2016).
James, J. (2016) 'Parent-Infant Psychotherapy in Groups.' In T. Baradon with M. Biseo, C. Broughton, J. James and A. Joyce *The Practice of Psychoanalytic Parent-Infant Psychotherapy: Claiming the Baby*. 2nd edn. London: Routledge.
Kraemer, S. (2016) 'The View from the Bridge: Taking a Third Position to Child Health.' In S. Campbell, R. Catchpole and D. Morley (eds) *Child & Adolescent Mental Health: New Insights to Practice*. London: Palgrave Macmillan.
NHS (2016) *Specialist Health Visitors in Perinatal and Infant Mental Health: What They Do and Why They Matter*. Available at: https://hee.nhs.uk/our-work/developing-our-workforce/nursing/specialist-health-visitors-perinatal-infant-mental-health (Accessed: 1 December 2016).
Perry, B.D. (2004) *Maltreated Children: Experience, Brain Development and the Next Generation*. 2nd edn. London: W.W. Norton.
Sleed, M., James, J., Baradon, T., Newbery, J. and Fonagy, P. (2013) 'A psychotherapeutic baby clinic in a hostel for homeless families: practice and evaluation.' *Psychology and Psychotherapy: Theory, Research and Practice 86*, 1, 1–18.

CHAPTER 3

The Eve Project –
Dancing with Baby

Supporting Young Families in the Community

Ruth Price

This chapter describes an emerging dance movement community project for first-time parents, highlighting their lived experiences during the influential developmental stage of the perinatal period.

A RATIONALE FOR PREVENTATIVE COMMUNITY PROJECTS

Research has conclusively demonstrated that the health of women and children is crucial for the development of thriving and stable societies.

(EVERY WOMAN, EVERY CHILD,
UNITED NATIONS FOUNDATION 2016)

At birth, love is not only an emotional requirement but a biological necessity for a baby. Without the cuddling and hugging an infant will literally wilt and die. ...this condition is called 'marasmus' ... and was until the early years of the twentieth century responsible for nearly 100% of the deaths in foundling homes.

(VERNY WITH KELLY 1982: 135)

Organizations such as the National Society for the Prevention of Cruelty to Children (Hogg 2013) and the World Health Organization (WHO 2015) all identify the vitally important role of maternal physical and mental health for the successful development of babies.

THE BEGINNING: IDENTIFYING THE NEED

The project was originally called the Eve project ('Eve' means 'life' in Hebrew), emphasizing the importance of the crucial first connection between a mother and her baby, which provides the foundation for all that is to follow in each individual's journey into adulthood.

An encounter with a mother who seemed startlingly dismissive of her own importance to her baby led me to look for local provisions for parents and babies. There were various activity groups, mostly run privately and therefore not available to those who could not afford to pay for them. The only council-funded local support group for parents and babies during the perinatal period was short term (up to six weeks) and could be accessed only via a general practitioner (GP) referral. There appeared to be a clear need for some provision, with a degree of therapeutic intentionality, which understood that early intervention is a powerful tool in reducing the impact of isolation and depression that often accompanies the arrival of a new baby.

THE RATIONALE

Winnicott identified that 'the baby needs the environmental stability that facilitates continuity of personal experience' (Winnicott, Winnicott and Davis 1986, p.147). This was the reason for providing a consistent level of support and interaction, which benefits both baby and parent.

INVOLVING FATHERS

Engaging fathers during the perinatal period, a time of crucial development, in the child's life, has been recognized as a critical factor in preventive intervention. Ramchandani *et al.* (2013, p.63) states that

'Disengaged and remote interactions between fathers and their babies at age 3 months independently predicted externalising behavioural problems at the age of 1 year.' The Eve project was successful in involving fathers as well as mothers. Several fathers came to the group in order to maintain continuity for the babies, as a result of maternal insistence – 'It's baby's favourite group!' (Eowen and Rianna) – rather than any requirement for consistent attendance by the group leader. Their interactions were noticeably more physically active than those of the mothers despite the dance context!

DEFINING THE PROJECT

After discussions with the local health visitor, staff at the children's centre and a colleague working to establish a neighbourhood parent support scheme, the Eve project was launched. Its aims were to:

- hold the ethos of a therapeutic movement and meeting group
- be facilitated as an open group
- target the 0–12-month age range
- be made available free of charge at the point of use.

PROMOTING THE PROJECT

The flyers, a website and invitation cards for health visitors and staff at the children's centre offered a group for music, movement and rhythms to encourage and explore different ways of connecting with babies, led by myself, a Registered Dance Movement Psychotherapist. It was a slow start and most of the parents who attended the group found their way in through word of mouth.

The very first mother who attended became instrumental in spreading the word around the first-time parents' group, and this established a strong core of eight to ten babies and their parents. A group page was established via Facebook, and connections and access to the group were increasingly promoted through social media and a local free paper.

METHODS

The format of the sessions had been piloted for three months with a twins support group, and had received unanimously positive feedback. Each session started with a physical warm-up and a check-in where participants could share their latest news and how they were feeling at that moment. There followed opportunities for some expressive movement, for shared or contrasting rhythms, and then a winding down to a closing circle and checking out, where participants could name any emerging thoughts, images or feelings. All of this would take place within the context of an eclectic range of music, supported by various props, such as silky fabrics, shakers and streamers.

The aim was to make space for *both* parent and baby and, in so doing, to enhance their interaction and experience through 'shared, reciprocal and pleasurable movement experiences' (Doonan and Bräuninger 2015, p.240).

SOOTHING

The movement activities helped parents to slow down, to identify and experiment with natural rhythms that soothed and satisfied their child. This had a profound impact on the relationships with their babies and with each other. They also discovered that their own needs for 'soothing' or for 'stimulation' were met in this process:

> I love the informal manner, it makes me feel relaxed...the music and dancing lifts my spirits and gives me a real sense of wellbeing. (Kathryn and Della)

> Baby Rianna gets the benefit ... she is all smiles during the group, then sleeps really well afterwards. (Eowen and Rianna)

> The music and movement helps me bond with E. I've noticed how it helps his development. (Kedzie and Ethan)

The activities we engaged in during the weekly Eve project sessions provided opportunities for facilitated and spontaneous sharing of lives.

ATTUNEMENT SUPPORTS ATTACHMENT

Stern comments on the dance of attunement between parent and child:

> First the parent must be able to read the baby's feeling state from the baby's overt behavior. Second, the parent must perform some behavior that is not a strict imitation but nonetheless corresponds in some way to the baby's overt behavior. Third, the baby must be able to read this corresponding parental response as having to do with the baby's own original feeling experience and not just imitating the baby's behavior. It is only in the presence of these three conditions that feeling states within one person can be knowable to another and that they *can both sense, without using language* that the transaction has occurred. (Stern 1991, p.139, my emphasis)

Vlismas, Malloch and Burnham add:

> 'Attunement' can also be described as awareness and sensing of another's emotional and physical rhythms. In the same way that a violin's strings will vibrate in response to another's strings being played if they are tuned to the same frequency, there is the same capacity in each of us to resonate with another's emotional and physical state. Within a mother and baby dyad this can provide invaluable support for nurturing attachment, and this reciprocity is enhanced by music and movement. (Vlismas, Malloch and Burnham 2013, p.1684)

My role as a Dance Movement Psychotherapist was that of nurturing and of structuring the group, using my ability to attune and to craft connections. My empathic awareness helped to foster a therapeutic, safe space within which parents and babies could discover joy in one another: 'It was lovely to have fun with my baby doing different activities we wouldn't ordinarily do!' (Kedzie and Ethan)

THE GROUP BECOMES A COMMUNITY

The numbers at each session varied between 4 and 14. Within the core membership there was an emerging sense of commitment and shared ownership. The original focus of the Eve project broadened over time. Even though my original intention was to encourage movement interactions, which supported the **resonance** between parents and babies, these developing skills also appeared to benefit other relationships within the group: 'The mums and babies we have met have become great friends' (Kate). Parents commented on feeling at home in the group, and they were therefore more prepared to develop new connections. The Eve project was slowly becoming a 'safe' place and a 'play' place.

The group began to form links that went beyond the weekly hour and a half session. They kept in touch through social media and exchanged mobile numbers in order to arrange to meet up for coffee. This progressed into regular group lunches after the sessions and members began to attend different activities together: 'Coming along here…it gave me a chance to mix and meet with people I wouldn't otherwise have any contact with. I like that' (Roxy).

A relational web was starting to emerge initiated by the Eve project.

Analysis of participants' feedback confirmed Doonan and Bräuninger's (2015) research. Parents stated that they loved 'The welcoming and relaxed atmosphere, the informal structure, fun for baby, fun for me, making new friends for baby and me, new ideas of how to "be" with baby, feeling safe.' (Eowen and Rianna)

Often, when grandparents happened to visit, or if partners had a day off work, they would be brought along and would join in with the rest of the group because no one wanted to miss what they considered to be the highlight of their week. On one occasion, one of the mothers collected Granny and Uncle from the airport and brought them too!

> Motherhood can feel a bit isolating so it's great to have a place like this…it feels like we're building a community. (Kate and Edie; Jasmine and Bradley)

Bertalanffy's systemic theory highlights the fact that even small changes can impact on the whole and vice versa (Rosen 1969). The Eve project constituted a small change in one group of parent-baby dyads, which had profound subsequent impact whose dimensions have not yet been completely captured. Further research is needed to identify the long-term effects of such early relational investment.

EXAMPLE

Finlay was born prematurely and underweight when he first started coming to the group. He was Harriet's first baby. She was anxious and extremely concerned about Finlay's weight. She seemed fast and constantly 'on the go', in a starting–stopping rhythm.

When Finlay was distressed, Harriet's soothing of him involved little high-speed bounces, stepping from side to side, with him held in her arms. My initial perception was that her rhythms seemed to 'clash' with those of the baby. Winnicott observed that 'failure of adaptation can be recognized and turned into adaptive success' (Winnicott 2014, p.147). Harriet noticed Finlay's responses in 'rainbow time', which is the closing part of the session with multi-coloured fabric and calming music. Finlay was soothed by the slower swaying rhythm and movement of the fabric that more closely matched his own.

Winnicott (1949) states that a 'good enough' mother can learn to provide a 'good enough' environment for her baby. Harriet's comment in the group was, 'I think I need to have some rainbow time with Finlay at home…he always loves it and gets really settled.' Harriet had adjusted her strategies and adapted her rhythms and become more attuned to her baby's patterns. It bodes well for their future relationship.

This is an example of 'parental embodied mentalizing' (Shai and Belsky 2011), which refers to the parent's capacity to perceive their baby's mood from their whole-body movement, and to then adjust their own patterns accordingly. This shift from mismatching to matching is part of the continuous interactional pattern of healthy development.

FEEDBACK AND OTHER OUTCOMES

Parents' feedback was unanimous in recognizing that the Eve project had supported them through that crucial post-partum year and had provided them with a sense of 'extended family' (Kate), 'just like when my mum would take me to see my favourite aunty' (Jasmine).

They appreciated slowing down and 'having time to reflect how things really are...without the normal rushing' (Kedzie and Ethan). They discovered that parenthood need not be a huge challenge that has to be faced alone. 'I can admit it now...I was depressed...the Eve project was a solid source of support for me' (Kate and Edie); 'I made friends for life' (Jasmine and Bradley). They were equally clear that the project had started something that they did not want to stop: 'I am having my second baby, I hope this group will carry on, I need it' (Catharine).

OTHER OUTCOMES: INVESTING IN THE FUTURE

As I write this, a new group of 0–12-month-old babies and their parents has started and the original group continues its adventure in building friendship and community together and in changing their experiences of isolation and inadequacy into a nurturing fellowship of resilience.

My desire to invest in early relationships prompted me to start the Eve project. This was only possible because I have given my time and skills for free along with two volunteer helpers. The only funding we have received so far is a donation that covers the hire of the hall.

The success of the Eve project underlines the need for provision of this kind within our communities. The argument for investing time and resources in this project is clear. Its sustainability will depend on funding training for other practitioners, attracting volunteers and involving parents as stakeholders. Research highlights the worthwhile impact of early intervention, which 'supports the development of a secure attachment between baby and caregiver' (Hogg 2013, p.14).

The interventions and the principles underlying the project were neither new nor unique. The efficacy of the Eve sessions lay, as ever, within the relationships that were forged. The Eve project has become a safe anchorage for the families, and I have come away richer, not poorer, for meeting them.

REFERENCES

Doonan, F. and Bräuninger, I. (2015) 'Making space for the both of us: how dance movement therapy enhances mother–infant attachment and experience.' *Body, Movement and Dance in Psychotherapy 10*, 4, 227–242.

Every Woman, Every Child (2016) *Global Strategy for Women's, Children's and Adolescents' Health (2016–2030)*. Available at: http://www.everywomaneverychild.org/resources/publications (Accessed: 21 December 2016).

Hogg, S. (2013) *Prevention in Mind: All Babies Count: Spotlight on Perinatal Mental Health*. London: NSPCC. Available at: https://www.nspcc.org.uk/globalassets/documents/research-reports/all-babies-count-spotlight-perinatal-mental-health.pdf (Accessed: 21 December 2016).

Ramchandani, P.G., Domoney, J., Sethna, V., Psychogiou, L., Vlachos, H. and Murray, L. (2013) 'Do early father–infant interactions predict the onset of externalising behaviours in young children? Findings from a longitudinal cohort study.' *Journal of Child Psychology and Psychiatry 54*, 1, 56–64.

Rosen, R. (1969) Review of *General System Theory. Foundations, Development, Applications*, by Ludwig von Bertalanffy. *Science 164*, 3880, 681–682.

Shai, D. and Belsky, J. (2011) 'When words just won't do: introducing parental embodied mentalizing.' *Child Development Perspectives 5*, 3, 173–180.

Stern, D.N. (1991) *The Interpersonal World of the Infant: A View from Psychoanalysis and Developmental Psychology; with a New Introduction by the Author*. New York: Basic Books.

United Nations Foundation (2014) *Every Woman, Every Child: A Post-2015 Vision: The Third Report of the Independent Expert Review Group on Information and Accountability for Women's and Children's Health*. Available at: http://apps.who.int/iris/bitstream/10665/132673/1/9789241507523_eng.pdf (Accessed: 5 December 2016).

Verny, T.R. with Kelly, J. (1982) *The Secret Life of the Unborn Child*. London: Sphere Books.

Vlismas, W., Malloch, S. and Burnham, D. (2013) 'The effects of music and movement on mother–infant interactions.' *Early Child Development and Care 183*, 11, 1669–1688.

Winnicott, D. W. (1949) 'Mind and Its Relation to the Psyche-soma.' In *Collected Papers: Through Pediatrics to Psycho-Analysis*. London: Tavistock.

Winnicott, D.W. (2014) in *Through Pediatrics to Psycho-analysis: Collected Papers*. London: Routledge.

Winnicott, D.W., Winnicott, C. and Davis, M. (1986) *Home Is Where We Start From: Essays by a Psychoanalyst*. Ed. Ray Shepherd. Harmondsworth: Penguin Books.

World Health Organization (2015) *The iERG 2015 Report*. Available at: http://www.who.int/woman_child_accountability/ierg/en/ (Accessed: 21 December 2016).

CHAPTER 4

Roots and Blossoms

A Children's Centre Role in Nurturing Groups for
Vulnerable Parents Starting in Pregnancy

Lisa Clayden, Cristina Franklin and Norma Thompson with Monika Celebi

This chapter describes the ethos of a children's centre and how staff
engaged vulnerable parents to attend groups from the perspective
of a children's centre manager. A midwifery community support
project, hosted on the premises, gives an example of working across
professional boundaries for the health and wellbeing of hard to reach
families in a welcoming community setting.

BACKGROUND

The children's centre was in an area with a transient, culturally and
socially diverse population. It was part of the Government Sure Start
initiative and the Ten Year Strategy for Childcare (2004). As manager,
I (Norma Thompson) was accountable to show we met targets set
by policy makers to receive funding. Our challenge was to evaluate
the multi-faceted and deeply human work of caring for the local
parents and babies and providing a safe space for them, in a required

format, which did not entirely capture the holistic nature of the care we provided.

NEW PARENTS OFTEN STRUGGLE

Our experience was that many new parents, even though they had access to a vast range of information, often felt they should be able to understand and manage their new role without help. They tended to mask their emotional struggles with concerns about their baby's sleeping and feeding. This was a concrete way of expressing their anxieties, but actually it often indicated possible underlying mental health concerns for either the baby or the parent (Daws 1989). Capturing a baseline when parents were still unaware of concerns was problematic when gathering evidence for the key performance indicators.

A WELCOMING ENVIRONMENT ENCOURAGES RELATIONSHIP BUILDING

Many families have described that it took courage to get through the door of the children's centre in the first place. As the manager of the centre, I felt it was important to create a clean, organized, warm and welcoming environment, with the consistent and encouraging presence of familiar team members. 'I think I attended the groups because all the staff supported me' (Alison).

THE CHILDREN CENTRE – A FRIENDLY SPACE FOR MANY DIFFERENT GROUPS

Baby Café, which supported breastfeeding, often was the first contact families had with the centre. We also provided Therapeutic Touch–baby massage groups (see Chapter 1) to promote **sensitive caregiving** between parents and babies through physical touch. If parents of older babies were seen to need further support, they were encouraged to attend therapeutic Baby Watching groups (see Chapter 7), led by an outside specialist, or referred to individual counselling sessions.

Softer groups, such as cooking and art-based therapy, helped families to make connections with each other. The practical elements of these groups allowed conversations to evolve without feeling the pressure of having to share personal information.

There were also groups for child minders, first aid, learning to cook, English as a Second Language (ESOL), early learning support, speech therapy, Adult Literacy and Numeracy, and Baby Massage for fathers, as well as a fathers' Forest School (subsidized outdoor activities for families in local nature reserves, city farms or allotments) and transition sessions for parents whose children were to attend school nurseries. Having universal services was crucial to identify when a family needed further help. 'Saplings' was a group for vulnerable expecting mothers, which was hosted alongside the universal stay and play sessions run by the centre.

Families had the opportunity when they came in to meet the midwife or health visitor, to see additional group sessions, without having to commit themselves to attending. Our aim was to engage parents who may have had poor experiences at school to experiment with attending a group. This gentle approach in turn often gave them confidence to subsequently attend other group activities, especially if the cohort moved on together. The children's centre itself became a friendly space, which parents attached to.

WHO SHOULD ATTEND A GROUP?

The children's centre provided an opportunity for staff to get to know parents and understand when they were ready to engage with a particular group. If a child lived in a household where there was domestic abuse and the child was part of a Child Protection Plan, there was often an urgency from the social worker to engage the parent, usually the mother, in attending a group to help her understand the impact of domestic abuse. Such pressure could be counterproductive. If a parent was forced to attend, their choice was taken away, and so they were likely to be resistant and often angry. This in turn would impact on the ambience of the whole group. The team therefore worked individually with parents to assess their readiness and the appropriateness of offering support in the form of group work, as inappropriate referrals for a family in crisis might lead to increased risk for the family and sabotage other group participants.

As a rule, groups benefitted from having a mix of people. Having a positive role model could increase others' hopefulness and confidence and increase the potential for the success of the group.

REFERRING INTO GROUPS AND ESTABLISHING CLEAR EXPECTATIONS

If invited to attend a parenting group or a group for postnatal depression, parents could feel stigmatized. The children's centre experimented with nondescript titles to avoid this issue but this also proved problematic. There needed to be clarity about the purpose of the group and who could or should attend.

A personal conversation to clarify the goals of the recommended group and an informal introduction to the relevant group facilitator was an important part of the groundwork. This helped create the message that this person could be trusted, and that the group was friendly and would be helpful. This approach allowed both self-referrals and professionals to signpost into the groups.

Staff would try to ensure that there was a flow and connection between groups by becoming a familiar face to the families and co-facilitating groups with outside specialists. Partnerships with schools, health visitors, midwives and local mental health organizations were also nurtured to create joined-up thinking and action. The following is an example of such a partnership with the local midwifery team.

THE SAPLINGS PROJECT – GROUP ANTENATAL CARE FOR CLIENTS WITH ADDITIONAL NEEDS

I (Lisa Clayden) am a community midwife. I facilitated the Saplings project, which provided antenatal care in a group setting to women with complex social vulnerabilities who have low levels of inter-action with education and support services. Many of the women had a history of mental ill-health, domestic abuse, isolation, substance abuse or learning difficulties, with some having had older children removed because of safeguarding concerns; some were victims of human trafficking and some were refugees. These women were at increased risk of postnatal depression and as a client group less likely to engage with care at all. Their babies subsequently had poorer health outcomes (Murray *et al.* 2003).

Our team included myself and an assistant practitioner; however, it was found that ideally it should be made up of two midwives. We worked closely with the children's centre staff, social services, the midwifery community team and other specialist agencies.

AIMS OF SAPLINGS

When a group of people come together for a common purpose of health and well-being, to share information and learn together, a transformation happens at both the personal and collective level that brings about better understanding, greater engagement, and self-confidence.

(Healthcare Institute 2009)

We wanted our clients to understand their own antenatal care and also to provide peer and professional support. A rolling programme covered a wide range of subjects and included labour and birth preparation, parenting, practical baby care, healthy lifestyle choices, nutrition, smoking cessation, housing benefits and availability of mental health services.

We always offered a drink and snack. Much-liked activities such as a short hand massage or making a plaster of Paris belly cast in the last few weeks of pregnancy were a light-hearted and gentle way to address the challenges of self-care and of changing bodies during pregnancy and early motherhood. A yoga and mindfulness practitioner visited once a month, but some clients found being still even for a minute challenging. Other specialists, such as health visitors and mental health professionals, came to give talks. A counsellor joined us to support thinking about the unborn baby. New parents returned and recounted their birth experiences.

ENGAGING FAMILIES

We had on average 30 women referred to the project at any given point and around 10 attending each week at the children's centre. Success in engaging women varied. Many were reluctant to answer the phone to an unfamiliar number. We found that women were more likely to engage with the group if we did the initial booking at their home. It often took several weeks of visits and phone calls before they finally came to the Centre. Once they attended, they usually enjoyed the experience. Frances, one of the mothers, told me, 'I was anxious before I came, but it's very friendly. Everyone talks to you. You make friends with women who have children the same age. It means you don't bore your friends who aren't pregnant.'

BEING OPEN AND FLEXIBLE

A core group of parents attended most weeks alongside others who came less regularly or only when they were due antenatal appointments. A few clients choose to have their care with the midwife at their GP surgery and attended Saplings as well. Groups were open to women of all gestations and their family members, and we also welcomed those who had already had their babies for as long as they needed. They often provided excellent role models for breastfeeding to the newly pregnant mothers. Flexibility was key in ensuring all clients had their choices respected.

REFLECTION

The transitory and shifting nature of the group made it at times seem chaotic but the welcoming, supportive and containing environment of the children's centre team helped to manage the multiplicity of needs. Women who struggled to attend regular clinic appointments said that they appreciated the regularity and social and emotional support

Saplings provided. High attendance rates confirmed this. 'Everyone is really close here; it's like a family; no one judges you' (Sandra).

ANTENATAL CHECKS

Women were offered antenatal checks either at the beginning or end of the session, which took place at one end of the room in a space symbolically separated by a screen. Group members could walk past this area and stop to ask questions. This was surprising to some, but others really enjoyed, for instance, sharing their baby's heartbeat. If a mother preferred a private room, this would always be respected. Our aim was to normalize the experience of pregnancy and prepare women for the physical contact with professionals during labour, as well as help to negotiate obstetric and midwifery care.

JOINING OTHER GROUP ACTIVITIES

Saplings operated concurrently with an open 'Stay and Play' session in the children's centre, and women would often move between the two groups. Alison, a young mother, had her first child removed by social services. When she gave birth to another baby, she was frightened that she would lose him too. Initially reluctant, she was encouraged to attend groups by the network of professionals in and around the children's centre. 'Once I came to Saplings,' she said, 'I really enjoyed it. I made friends and we went on to do other groups.'

REFLECTION

Friendly relationships between the Saplings team and the children's centre staff helped to extend the support and safety net for Saplings families, postnatally. This joined-up approach encouraged women's attendance of other groups for which they received priority, and allowed for continuity of care. 'Baby Massage and Baby Watching brought me closer to my baby. I wish I had that with my first child. Afterwards I felt more confident to try other groups. I think I enjoyed the practical bit of the cooking group, learning to give my child healthy food,' Alison reflected. Alison later went on to attend the domestic abuse support group, which ran in the children's centre.

PREVENTION

Anna, a young, heavily pregnant parent new to the area, attended the universal play and stay sessions with her two-year-old. She seemed well attuned to her child yet was highly agitated. I (Cristina Franklin) recognized this as a possible symptom of a hidden problem and after some individual conversations, invited her to attend the Women's Group, which ran alongside a crèche. The group ran without an agenda to allow women the opportunity to talk freely, share their week, give and receive support and also to offer their children a quality play experience. The atmosphere in the group was open and friendly and allowed laughter and tears to be shed in equal measure.

Anna felt safe to raise her concerns about her partner, against whom an allegation of inappropriate behaviour towards a child had been made. Staff then supported her to contact social services. The eventual outcome was that Anna left the man, who was unsafe for her children.

I was alerted to this mother because we all had been trained to be observant of child development and parent-baby interactions. In weekly reflective team meetings we thought about all the families who attended the universal services and highlighted any particular concerns. This prevention strategy allowed us to reach vulnerable parents before their family situation deteriorated, and became a crisis and therefore more damaging to the child.

Parents such as Anna fed back to the team that they would not have attended a group and shared their unhappiness unless they had been personally invited and made to feel safe to disclose their concerns. Being able to notice distress in the universal play sessions and to gradually build up a relationship with vulnerable parents made the invitation and attendance at the women's group possible.

CONCLUSIONS

It is the opinion of the authors that without universal playgroups and children's centres open to all, vulnerable families are in danger of slipping through the net of social care. Many mothers who attended the centre had no relatives nearby and were living in isolation. They looked to the children's centre for support and advice especially when their first child was born. Isolation increases the risk of mental illness, child neglect and abuse (WAVE Trust 2015). Carol, who initially had not dared to leave her house said, 'The children's centre had become my second home.'

We needed both trained staff and opportunities to spot early warning signs, to avoid problems becoming entrenched, more damaging and harder to repair (WAVE Trust 2015). In the children's centre, which was open to all, vulnerable parents who may not meet the official thresholds for additional support benefitted from the grounding environment and its dedicated workforce, who provided a **secure base** for nurturing the next generation.

Engaging parents effectively is a complex process, as each person has a different history, concerns, fears and needs. The children's centre supported parents to feel safe by making them welcome, listening to them and understanding when they might be ready to attend a group or discuss concerns. Universal services provided a non-stigmatized point of entry for those who needed to test the provision, before signalling that they could ask for and accept help. The children's centre provided a containing space, which encouraged group attendance. This demanded sensitivity, perseverance, and open channels of communication between families and the different professionals, to build a support system in the community, which improved outcomes for children and babies.

Sadly the children's centre described here has been identified for closure, as a result of budget cuts.

REFERENCES

Daws, D. (1989) *Through the Night: Helping Parents with Sleepless Infants*. London: Free Association Books.

Healthcare Institute (2009) 'CenteringPregnancy.' Available at: https://www.centeringhealthcare.org/what-we-do/centering-pregnancy (Accessed: 5 December 2016).

Murray, L., Woolgar, M., Murray, J. and Cooper, P. (2003) 'Self-exclusion from health care in women at high risk for postpartum depression.' *Journal of Public Health 25*, 2, 131–137.

WAVE Trust (2015) *Building Great Britons*. Available at: http://www.wavetrust.org/our-work/publications/reports/building-great-britons (Accessed: 5 December 2016).

CHAPTER 5

VIMA (Step)

A Greek Early Intervention Programme Promoting Attachment
between Parents and Children to Prevent Abuse and Neglect

*Korina Hatzinikolaou, Katerina Ydraiou, Eleni
Agathonos, Myrto Nielsen and Klio Geroulanou*

SUMMARY

This chapter charts the development of VIMA, an early intervention
programme in inner city Athens, which started as one group, to discuss
early child development issues, initially with no youngsters present,
up until the time of writing when VIMA offered a parent-baby and
toddler group, a **parent-baby and toddler cooking group**, individual
and family counselling and additional services. The children's
ages range from nought to five years. The process of transforming
the programme according to the community's needs as well as the
interventions are discussed.

BACKGROUND

'VIMA' means 'step' in Greek, and it is the name of a group-based early
intervention programme for native and immigrant parents of infants
and toddlers, carried out by two nongovernmental organizations
(NGOs) in Athens. It is one of only a few such programmes currently
offered to new parents and families at risk for child maltreatment,

who also experience economic, political and financial hardship. Participating families are from Greece as well as refugees from African and Asian countries, most of whom have been living in Athens for a couple of years and whose children were born in Greece. All families face increased challenges as a result of the financial crisis that has affected Greece. VIMA has been developed through a dialogic process with the community.

INTRODUCTION

Over the last 50 years Greece has been undergoing multiple changes affecting its economic, ethnic and social fabric. Internal migration has decreased the likelihood of keeping together the 'traditional' extended family, while the emerging nuclear family has had to adapt to the reality of social isolation, single parenthood and divorce. The opening of the borders with Greece's neighbouring countries in the early 1990s was followed by large populations of migrants and, currently, refugees from Africa, Asia and the Middle East, which the country was not ready to integrate and therefore it was not ready to adjust to the new situation. Athens, as the capital, drew the greatest number of internal and foreign migrants, and local communities were quickly transformed into multi-ethnic niches. Although the centre of Athens is still home to many Greek families, a considerable number of migrant and refugee families from Africa (Nigeria, Kenya, Egypt), Southeast Asia (Afghanistan, Bangladesh) and the Middle East (Syria, Iraq) also reside there.

Central Athens is home to our organization, One Child, One World. We observed that, while immigrant, refugee and Greek families share the same public spaces, the same kindergartens and the same cafes, they are not systematically offered a common space to discuss issues such as being a healthy family. Our programme, VIMA, has offered this opportunity; however, a lot of work on establishing quality cultural communication between Greek and immigrant families is still needed. The State, which owing to the present systemic socio-economic crisis has cut much social welfare provision, practically leaves family units to provide the bedrock of society. At the same time, civil society, through its NGOs, is attempting to support the State in providing basic social services. Often the NGOs replace the State's role.

In such times of political and economic uncertainties, the equilibrium of risk factors versus protective factors is challenged (Agathonos-Georgopoulou and Browne 1997). Parenting babies and toddlers becomes even more difficult when families lack support, and the risk for child abuse and/or maltreatment greatly increases. Providing opportunities to new parents for positive experiences is especially crucial, as they contribute to the mending of the social fabric when it is broken. In Greece, early intervention was recognized and promoted from the beginning of the 21st century (Nakou, Stathakopoulou and Agathonos 1987).

VIMA was implemented in 2013 with the aim of supporting parents of babies and toddlers. It developed into a more comprehensive early intervention programme including family counselling, parent-baby/ toddler groups, other group interventions as well as community outreach. VIMA is the outcome of the collaboration between One Child, One World and the NGO, ELIZA – Society for the Prevention of Cruelty to Children; both these NGOs are based in Athens. VIMA is innovative for Greek standards, as it offers the community a range of parenting support services, which are cost-free and open even to families who don't receive help from the Greek national social security system.

PLANNING AND ESTABLISHING
THE VIMA PROGRAMME

VIMA was designed according to the ethical grounds of the United Nations Convention on the Rights of the Child (UN 1989) and is based on systemic and attachment theory, as well as basic principles of social justice. The programme initially developed a step-by-step approach and advanced on the basis of an ongoing dialogic process with the community. Its development included:

- in-service training through staff, clinical meetings as well as training events and seminars

- organizational as well as clinical supervision by experienced external supervisors

- relevant literature review, formulation of a theoretical model and the design of interventions, overseen by a scientific interdisciplinary committee who met bi-monthly

- liaising with other community services and NGOs

- recruitment of volunteers (preferably from relevant professional fields)

- production and organization of promotional material to be used in the community.

INITIAL IMPLEMENTATION AND LATER DEVELOPMENTS OF THE VIMA PROGRAMME

REMIT OF THE PROGRAMME

During its pilot phase, VIMA aimed at understanding the multiple needs of families with children from nought to five years of age who were already obtaining social support and services from the two NGOs that had established VIMA. This facilitated accessing families in need.

REFERRAL SOURCES AND CRITERIA

Referrals to VIMA come from NGOs, community baby and child mental health centres, maternity hospitals, kindergartens and nurseries. In many cases, referrers' initial work is to encourage the family to acknowledge their needs and seek help. The inclusion criteria are adverse childhood experiences and clinical concerns about parents' bond with their child. The programme's exclusion criteria involve substance misuse, severe clinical psychopathology and children diagnosed with a developmental disorder or threating illnesses. These we feel are dealt with more efficiently by other more specialized services.

SERVICES OFFERED

Two psychologists at VIMA provide counselling to parents, families and groups. In parallel they extend their services to raise community awareness of the importance of the early years of babies' lives. Services are free and offered in both Greek and English.

INITIAL GROUP WORK

Initially VIMA professionals offered parents small weekly support groups without a clear-cut agenda. Each meeting lasted approximately two hours. The groups were co-facilitated and delivered in English. Central themes arising were: having 'quality time' for mothers, dealing with challenging behaviour, learning effective parenting strategies, and coping with poverty and other adversities such as being a single immigrant mother.

Many mothers were isolated and asked for help with child care. In response VIMA recruited, trained and supervised volunteers to look after the babies and toddlers while their mothers participated in the parenting groups. We then identified that childcare time could equally be used as a chance to promote the psychosocial development of babies and toddlers, through play and social interaction. Attendance at separate groups helped mothers and babies to learn to manage short-term separations.

The adult groups gave mothers opportunities to recount harrowing stories such as exploitation, incarceration and abandonment by partners, to name just a few. The group seemed to create a supportive community, and was felt by participants to be a reparative experience.

The staff observed mothers starting to think about their babies' and toddlers' emotional state and understand how they as parents had an impact on their behaviour and feelings. The mothers shared their worries about keeping their children safe, as well as being able to meet their basic needs. Positive changes were also witnessed in mother-baby and mother-toddler relationships. The group leaders felt that a lot of the group's time was taken up with mothers managing separation from their youngsters, however, and so following discussions and reflections in supervision, the VIMA model changed.

LATER DEVELOPMENTS IN GROUP WORK

Later developments in VIMA's group work include the implementation of **parent-toddler groups** and parent-baby and toddler cooking groups.

PARENT-TODDLER GROUPS

In spring 2014, VIMA started to pilot parent-baby and toddler groups (along the lines of the Anna Freud Centre's parent-toddler groups) whose main aim was to provide support for parents and toddlers around central emotional issues of this period. These groups are steady, deal with typical toddlers' behaviours and enable parents to come together and support each other. They run for a maximum of two years and are led by trained professionals following a psychoanalytic developmental approach (Woods and Pretorius 2011). During 2014, three such groups were delivered within VIMA to immigrants as well as to Greek families with children from one to four years of age.

PARENTS' VIEWS

During ending group sessions, parents were asked to share their experience and give verbal feedback. Parents evaluated positively: belonging to the group, getting support from each other as well as the facilitators, learning how to play, learning to manage behavioural difficulties through modelling as well as providing their youngsters with a safe space where they could meet and interact with others. Parents whose children were not at kindergarten or nursery evaluated this opportunity especially highly. Many parents felt the group helped their children adjust to kindergarten or nursery more easily.

PROFESSIONALS' EXPERIENCE

Professionals observed that, during this type of intervention, parents started to noticed their youngsters more and became more understanding of their toddlers' reactions, needs and wishes. Parents started to support their toddlers to verbalize feelings as well as to manage short-term separations. This type of intervention seemed also to encourage fathers' participation more, in comparison with the **open discussion groups**. This was possibly due to the 'play' nature of the group.

Families with children up to three years old seemed to benefit more from this type of intervention than families with older children. This is in line with the original parent-toddlers' group model (Navridi 2010; Woods and Pretorius 2011). VIMA professionals now stick to the age protocol when offering this type of intervention.

Mothers with significant mental health difficulties (e.g. clinical depression) found it hard to use the groups to their full extent as being expected to play with their children proved to be a challenging task for them; however, they too benefitted from the groups' supportive environment.

It was felt that this type of intervention allowed for more culturally sensitive practices – in comparison with open groups – as more concrete beliefs around parenting practices such as physical punishment came to light more easily during group 'down time'. This gave opportunities for discussion, offering alternative strategies and, it was hoped, creating new ways of managing upset toddlers.

PARENT-BABY AND TODDLER COOKING GROUP

In 2013, an additional type of multi-level group intervention was initiated to involve mothers who were not so psychologically minded and would not engage successfully in traditional counselling. Three such groups have taken place. Their main aim is to promote healthy family relationships by enhancing positive interaction. Cooking was chosen to be the main activity. Its special symbolic meaning to mother-child dyads was enhanced by group leaders drawing knowledge from participants' cultural identity and heritage.

During cooking group time children aged one to four years old have opportunities to play with and explore cooking ingredients. This promotes their cognitive development such as mathematics, comprehension and sensory skills. For example, toddlers are asked to measure cups of sugar or flour, name fruits and vegetables, as well notice how they look and taste. Cooking with mothers was highly enjoyed by all babies and toddlers, who were forbidden at home to enter the kitchen, as it was not seen to be safe. Cooking proved one of the everyday activities mothers and children could enjoy together.

The group ended each meeting with a shared meal. This, apart from the apparent symbolic community-building function, also provided opportunities for fruitful discussions concerning diversity, racism, motherhood and parenting and became the venue for working through group dynamics. At the end of the group a cooking book with all the recipes with relevant photos was given to participants to serve as a group memento.

MOTHERS' VIEWS

During ending group sessions, mothers were asked to share their experience and give verbal feedback. Mothers greatly valued this type of group as it was experienced as highly enjoyable, lively and empowering. Mothers appreciated getting positive time out from home with their youngsters, belonging to a steady and accepting group where they could interact, share and learn new things together, as well as dealing with issues around their family's integration and cultural identity.

PROFESSIONALS' EXPERIENCE

We felt that in the cooking group, more than any other, youngsters seemed to belong more to the group than to their mothers solely.

This was facilitated by the group's open format, which enabled socializing significantly. It seemed that mothers trusted each other more quickly, looked after each other's infants and toddlers more directly, and shared positive observations about them. They all enjoyed feeding them. Cooking also allowed mothers to celebrate each family's cultural heritage as mothers taught the group traditional dishes from their country of origin.

Reflecting during supervision we thought about mothers' mental state as well as how attachment styles improved through modelling, sharing common worries around parenting, being supported by other mothers, having problem-free discussions as well as belonging to a steady group. The cooking group allowed for an indirect processing of all of the above issues in a stress-free environment.

WHERE ARE WE NOW?

At the time of writing VIMA has received an additional grant to continue implementing multi-family group interventions as they have proven to be an effective way of promoting attachment while supporting parents in the community.

Our current approach favours joint parent-baby and toddler groups, with play or activities such as cooking, to promote positive interaction between family members. This also responds to VIMA's secondary aim to prevent harshness towards babies and toddlers. In many cases, however, additional interventions are needed to support vulnerable families in more comprehensive ways.

In summary, the single best practice stemming from the various group interventions tested involved providing parents with a novel space where they could support each other, learn from each other and feel listened to. Respecting parents' own stories seems to enable them to acknowledge the experiences of their babies and toddlers as well as becoming more open to making use of alternative strategies when suggested.

We found that parents were able to start processing their toddlers' negative reactions only when they had been able to talk about the way their parents had parented them. This seemed to be the case independently of the type of intervention used, or the cultural background.

Parents' experiences differed somewhat in relation to group participation and process. For example, immigrant families seemed to feel more comfortable in the group settings compared with Greek ones. This should not result in a de facto separation of the two populations, however. We found that additional outdoor activities as a group, as well as art therapy activities and **mentalization** exercises promoted **psychological mindedness**, group cohesion as well as social integration in more direct ways.

FURTHER DEVELOPMENTS OF THE VIMA PROGRAMME

IMPACT ON THE COMMUNITY

VIMA's ethos is listening to users' voices and letting their needs inform VIMA's choice of services in a continuous effort to support new parents in the community, in ways that are meaningful to them. Community prevention and early intervention programmes create a 'therapeutic cradle' for vulnerable families to deal safely with the everyday difficulties of managing a young child. They create a social space for families with young children who face social exclusion and adverse life conditions. There, families can grow socially together and be empowered to become a community. Community programmes such as VIMA also respond to the increased social demand for mental health services for families with young children, which are currently lacking in Greece.

VIMA provides systemic community interventions, which increase social cohesion and raise the level of awareness about the importance of the early years for children's future development. Families are now informed by neighbours through word-of-mouth to approach VIMA directly for help.

My friend and neighbour, Ms. H., told me that she was getting mad and she was beating her child. But then, she came here and you helped her to stop doing it. That's why I came! (Joy)

We learned the importance of listening to our community, to take a reflective stance supported by supervision and to provide suitable practical and emotional early intervention services. We also discovered that many of the families attending the parent-baby and toddler groups already have established relationship problems. Hence, VIMA is now expanding its services to provide a group service exclusively for mothers with infants from nought to one year of age and home visiting.

Mental health services for families with children from nought to five years of age are especially scarce in rural areas and on the Greek islands. Further funding is being sought to implement the VIMA programme on three Greek islands, using the experience gained by VIMA, as a 'mobile incubator', to continue strengthening the social fabric of multi-ethnic neighbourhoods and increase help for more families that may need it.

REFERENCES

Agathonos-Georgopoulou, H. and Browne, K.D. (1997) 'The prediction of child maltreatment in Greek families.' *Child Abuse & Neglect 21*, 8, 721–735.

Nakou, S., Stathakopoulou, N. and Agathonos, H. (1987) 'Socio-cultural change and child abuse: implications for prevention.' Paper presented at the 1st European Conference on Child Abuse and Neglect, Rhodes (Abstracts).

Navridi, E. (2010) 'Integration, Sharing and Separation: Introducing the Concept of Toddlers and Toddler Groups in Greece.' In M.Z. Woods and I.-M. Pretorius (eds) *Parents and Toddlers in Groups: A Psychoanalytic Developmental Approach*. New York: Taylor & Francis.

United Nations (UN) (1989) *Convention on the Rights of the Child 1989*. Available at: http://www.ohchr.org/en/professionalinterest/pages/crc.aspx (Accessed: 5 December 2016).

Woods, M.Z. and Pretorius, I.-M. (eds) (2011) *Parents and Toddlers in Groups: A Psychoanalytic Developmental Approach*. London: Routledge.

USING VIDEO TO ENHANCE ATTUNEMENT

CHAPTER 6

Fun with Mum

Strengthening the Bonds Loosened by Postnatal Depression

Bridget Macdonald and Penny Rackett

Fun with Mum is a brief, group intervention for mothers with postnatal depression and their babies, using Video Interaction Guidance (VIG). It has been running for six years in various children's centres in Suffolk.

VIDEO INTERACTION GUIDANCE

VIG is a relationship-based intervention (Kennedy, Landor and Todd 2011) that uses video clips of real situations. By being shown, and reflecting on, moments of attunement, people are empowered to build on their strengths to develop the best possible relationships with those they love.

THE VIG PROCESS

The guider (the person who engages with the client and leads the process is called the VIG practitioner; shortened throughout this chapter to 'practitioner') films everyday interaction and chooses three clips on the basis that they show moments of connection between the parent and child; that the parent is following the child's lead; and that the clip illustrates a successful example of what the parent wants to work on. For instance, one of Claire's objectives for VIG work was 'To have more confidence in myself as a mum.' On a scale of 0–10 (0 = no confidence and 10 = full confidence) she placed herself on a 3, stating, 'I don't have a bond with Eliza, I'm not keeping her safe and I'm not protecting her.' Therefore the practitioner always showed clips where she could see herself as a competent, protective mother.

THE SHARED REVIEW

The clips are discussed together with the practitioner, who helps the parent identify how what they are doing might be making their child think and feel; and what the impact is on them both. Difficulties are explored as well as strengths. From microanalysis of seconds of interaction, deep understanding can occur. Claire's light bulb moment was realizing that she did not need to 'try' any more: all her life, she had been trying to please everyone and be accepted. It was an epiphany for her that she could tune in to herself as a competent parent and was able to see how her daughters responded to her. She was then able to focus on the interactions between herself and her children, trust her inner judgement, rather than listening to everyone around her.

VIG PRINCIPLES AND VALUES

Every part of Fun with Mum embodies the principles and values of VIG, not just the filming and shared reviews. So everything that is said and done by the facilitators reflects the Principles of Attuned Interaction and Guidance: being attentive, encouraging initiatives, receiving initiatives, developing attuned relationships, guiding and deepening the discussion (Kennedy *et al.* 2011); and the values of the Association for Video Interaction Guidance UK (AVIGuk 2011): respect, trust, hope, compassion, co-operation, appreciation, connection and empathy.

FUN WITH MUM

POSTNATAL DEPRESSION

Postnatal depression describes a worrying level of low mood identified in the weeks and months after the birth of a child. The causes can relate to recent events, such as a traumatic birth, but are often linked to earlier experiences of trauma, abusive relationships and long-term mental health difficulties. Claire grew up surrounded by violence and abusive language between her family members, and towards Claire; she had a sister whom her mother favoured, while Claire was constantly criticized. She told us: 'All I did was try to be liked. But whatever I did, it was never enough.'

Depression in the parent is a huge challenge for a baby, because their development depends on their carer's ability to observe them and offer attuned responses appropriate to their needs (Bowlby 1969). Initially Claire was so badly affected that she was continually tearful and didn't know what was happening from hour to hour. Her daughter would come to her, but Claire was so preoccupied with what was happening in her life she did not have space in her mind for her daughter. Both mother and baby needed understanding and a compassionate response at this crucial moment.

COLLABORATION IS AT THE HEART OF THE GROUP

The group was formed through collaboration between a social worker (Bridget Macdonald), an educational psychologist (Penny Rackett), a family support worker (Karen Papworth) and other key members of a children's centre. Bridget had found that 30–35 per cent of family support work requests involved depression, including postnatal depression, given as one of the main reasons for wanting help (the national average is 10 per cent [Hogg 2013]). Collaboration with the local health visiting team was essential. Julie Collins, a local health visitor, remembers seeing straightaway how the group would fill an urgent local need to address the impact of postnatal depression and to promote attachment.

REFERRALS

Mothers are either referred by their health visitor, following their initial postnatal visit, through family support, or identified through attending another group. Approximately one-third of the attending parents received support with housing, debt, attending appointments, domestic violence or other issues; or their child could be part of a Team Around the Child/Child in Need/Child Protection process. The mother might be referred to a counsellor, who would see her without her baby. The babies in the groups were usually aged less than six months to up to two years old.

BUILDING TRUST BEFORE THE GROUP STARTS

Each mother is visited at home prior to committing to the group: there she experiences the worker as being attentive, encouraging and receiving her initiatives. By being heard, and being asked about what she would like to get from the group, she can feel hopefulness about coming along.

ORGANIZATION OF THE GROUP

The group runs weekly over seven weeks and is structured sensitively to maximize a sense of safety and **containment**, where trust can be built and shared. Following an introductory group, each 1 hour 45 minute session is structured to offer time for mothers and babies to arrive and settle, followed by a circle time where thoughts are shared about their previous week and their feelings on that day. This experience of being encouraged to take initiatives and being received, key Principles of Attuned Interaction and Guidance (Kennedy *et al.* 2011), continues to be expressed and embodied by the facilitators in the group.

NURTURING THE PARENTS

Healthy snacks and a drink are prepared for each session with the facilitators serving these refreshments with care. Small pieces of quality dark chocolate are also offered to enhance the mothers' mood.

Guided relaxation forms part of two sessions, with the babies lying quietly with their mother or gently cradled by staff.

THE ROLE OF CIRCLE TIME

This can often be a very emotional time for some parents as they share their pain from the previous week and their struggles to cope. It is important to name these issues and acknowledge the impact of postnatal depression on their lives and relationships.

At the end of each session mothers share thoughts and feelings about the session in circle time, and celebrate their experiences from the shared review, when they reflected on positive images of themselves. The process of sharing their insights with the rest of the group enables them to try out and cement their ideas. It also allows them to re-experience the elation and test out this realization with the group, made up of people who are safe, receptive and attuned. This was particularly important for Claire, as she had been in unsafe relationships her entire life, with people who were not attuned to her and absorbed with their own feelings and thoughts. When Claire had her 'epiphany' about not needing to try any more, she told everyone at circle time with huge relief and elation. It was important for her to share this insight with the group; and a reflection on the group that she felt safe and supported to share this moment of inner realization.

PLANNED INTERACTION

A playful experience that involves a parent-child interaction is the focus of each week's activity and includes making individual treasure baskets, sensory play, messy play, reading stories or singing together. It is during these activities that the workers comment on how the babies and toddlers are responding to the activities – often they speak as if for them. For example: 'Oh, look Michelle at how he puts his hands out in such an excited way when you show him that yellow rattle.' The focus is always the contact between the mother and child, as opposed to a toy: 'Oh how Jayden's looking at your eyes, while you rattle that toy! He loves looking at you!' Another example is facilitators noticing and commenting on successful interactions: 'How Lucy loves you giving her space to explore the bear!'

Some parents like Emily appreciate the way that the group offers all the mothers the opportunity 'to enjoy their babies, do nice activities and have emotional support as and when they needed it'. She valued understanding better which activities helped babies to learn. She also talked about how these activities helped her to understand the things that Lizzie liked doing.

INDIVIDUAL TIME – EMPOWERMENT THROUGH SEEING ATTUNEMENT

We thought it was important to give mothers with postnatal depression individual time, so they could have a more intense experience of being attuned to by us. Moreover, it would give them more time in a safe space to explore deeply held beliefs about their internal working models (the patterns for how people view themselves, others and the world around them, that are created through relationships in infancy [Bowlby 1969]), which are affecting their relationships with their children.

We therefore shared their films in private rooms, on a one-to-one basis, withdrawing them from the group. Locally there is no parent-infant psychotherapy available and the adult mental health services are extremely stretched. Fun with Mum is often the only therapeutic parent-baby input received.

It was when Emily saw the video clips of moments of vitality and attunement between herself and her baby Lizzie that she was empowered to start to recover. She felt that she had always loved Lizzie but seeing the bond made them closer: 'I felt in myself that I believed it.' Understanding that by just being with her – cuddling her, touching her and talking to her gently about what was going on around them – she could make Lizzie very happy, was a powerful experience of attunement and emotional connection for Emily.

For Michelle, the attuned moments of interaction she saw on the video between her and Robbie were evidence of a developing sensitivity to his cues and needs, creating moments of emotional intimacy and shared pleasure. These moments gave Robbie the message that she was 'in touch' with him (Trevarthen 2004).

MANAGING AND CONTAINING STRONG FEELINGS

Feelings can be overwhelming. It has been said that babies have a sense of 'falling forever' when they do not feel emotionally attuned to and 'contained'. Mothers with postnatal depression can be overwhelmed by their own strong feelings, which may interfere with them being fully available to their babies. In Claire's individual sessions, Karen was able to receive Claire's feelings and show her how she was able to receive her daughter Eliza's emotions and respond appropriately. Karen helped her to see when she was able to read Eliza's cues, which linked back to her 'helping question' (to have more confidence in being a parent). In turn, Claire was able to respond sensitively to other parents in the group when they shared their difficult feelings. This shows how VIG works: experiencing attunement from the practitioner enables people to grow psychologically, be resourceful and discover their own resilience. It takes place within an interaction and has an impact on all that person's subsequent interactions. For Claire, this experience of being contained and seeing how she contained others was a significant stage in her journey.

SUPPORTING MENTALIZATION

By naming the moments of successful interaction between the mother and her child captured on video, the VIG practitioner helps each parent to explore what they and their child might be feeling and thinking, and so develop their capacity for **mentalization** (Fonagy, Gergely and Jurist 2005). Emily, after being shown attuned interactions with her daughter, was enabled by Bridget (practitioner) to wonder what was going on for her baby. She then began to talk more to Lizzie, asking her what she felt or thought, which in turn increased the moments of attuned contact between them.

When Ben was clearly uncomfortable and protesting, Bridget asked Lisa gently, 'I wonder if he would like to sit on this cushion?' Lisa was then able to consider how Ben was feeling and moved him. Another time, Ben's eyes were drooping, he had flopped onto the floor and looked unhappy, so Bridget quietly spoke for him, 'I'm sleepy, mummy, I need a cuddle.' Lisa was then able to pick him up.

When Josh (nine months old) cried, and his mother Emma was not responding, Penny asked, 'Is there anything we could help you with?' and this prompted Emma to think about what Josh needed – in this case, he was hungry and she fed him.

REFLECTIONS AND IMPACT

By reviewing the mother's targets we enable them to reflect on their own development and further embed the process of change. When Claire looked back on her VIG clips with Karen, she could see that she was initially 'acting at being a good mum' and found this extremely upsetting. But she was able to reflect on just how far she had come in her relationship with her daughter. At the same time, she was also able to see that even at her lowest point, she was able to protect her daughter.

For her VIG targets, she then placed herself at a 10 on the 0–10 scale, stating, 'Eliza looks up to me, relies on me to support her and to guide her,' and, 'I can feel we have good communication. I saw it, so now I believe it and I love her.' Before, Claire could say that she loved Eliza, but taking part in Fun with Mum, especially working with the film, brought about a crucial shift in feelings, enabling her to know herself and her daughter on a much deeper level and she started to believe in herself as capable parent.

Emily described how she and Lizzie have been 'really close since' and she still stays in touch with the other group members. Michelle told Bridget, 'I still look at it [the DVD of films clips] sometimes and see how far I've come now.' She described the whole experience as 'one of those incredible journeys' and feels that the whole family are happier now. She said, 'I interact with feeling now, whereas before I was going through the motions.' Michelle's target rating scores for her lack of confidence as a parent improved by 7.5 points (from 2 to 9.5), and was also 6 points up for feeling emotionally closer to baby Robbie and for understanding him better (from 4 to 10). Her postnatal depression score fell 10 points.

EVALUATION

Mothers evaluate the sessions at the end of each block, which informs improvements and development for following groups. In 2014, an audit of 22 completed sets of outcome measurements for the group demonstrated that the depression scores for 21 of the mothers had reduced, and that all the targets for 100 per cent of the parents had shown improvements (Rackett and Macdonald 2014).

Karina (the children's centre manager) was impressed by the parents' feedback; she thought that the group allowed mothers to feel that postnatal depression could be an acceptable part of the journey into parenthood. By normalizing the experience of postnatal depression, it enabled them to take the first step to recovery. She remembers hearing 'giggles' coming from the room; she understood that there was fun and laughter as well as hard work going on. She described the group as giving mothers hope and as offering 'an invisible thread of safety'.

Feedback from Julie (the health visitor) said that the Fun with Mum group enabled parents to become more confident and less isolated, and to improve their relationships with their babies, their mental health and their ability to communicate with others in the community. Other members of the health teams also reported that they saw the value of the group in the area and how it helped to ease their work load by supporting mothers when they needed it.

FUTURE JOURNEY

We have found that both the VIG film work together with the group experience of Fun with Mum, where everything is based on the Principles of Attuned Interaction and Guidance, helps parents to connect with their hearts and minds. It means that change in mother-baby relationships is possible, even when the parents feel desperate, and cannot see a way out. It helps mothers to start their journey into a more joyful future.

REFERENCES

Association for Video Interaction Guidance UK (AVIGuk) (2011) 'What is Video Interaction Guoidance?' Available at: http://www.videointeractionguidance. net/resources/Documents/SUPERVISOR%20RESOURCES/ITC/ ITC%20Handouts%208.16/handout%201%20Day%201.pdf (Accessed: 21 December 2016).

Bowlby, J. (1969) *Attachment and Loss: Vol. 1: Attachment.* 2nd edn. London: Hogarth Press and the Institute of Psycho-Analysis.

Fonagy, P., Gergely, G. and Jurist, E. (2005) *Affect Regulation, Mentalization, and the Development of the Self.* New York: Other Press.

Hogg, S. (2013) *Prevention in Mind: All Babies Count: Spotlight on Perinatal Mental Health.* London: NSPCC. Available at: https://www.nspcc.org.uk/globalassets/ documents/research-reports/all-babies-count-spotlight-perinatal-mental-health.pdf (Accessed: 21 December 2016).

Kennedy, H., Landor, M. and Todd, L. (eds) (2011) *Video Interaction Guidance: A Relationship-Based Intervention to Promote Attunement, Empathy and Wellbeing.* Philadelphia: Jessica Kingsley Publishers.

Rackett, P. and Macdonald, B. (2014) '"Fun with Mum": Using Video Interaction Guidance to enhance early relationships and diminish maternal postnatal depression.' *Educational and Child Psychology Journal 31,* 4, 82–92.

Trevarthen, C. (2004) 'Learning about ourselves, from children: why a growing human brain needs interesting companions?' 乳幼児発達臨床センター年報 =*Research and Clinical Center for Child Development Annual Report 26,* 9–44.

CHAPTER 7

A Friendly Mirror

Combining Watch, Wait and Wonder with Video
Interaction Guidance in Baby Watching Groups

Monika Celebi

This chapter describes Baby Watching groups, wherein I combine
Watch, Wait and Wonder with Video Interaction Guidance. I developed
this approach over a period of five years, during which I facilitated
14 groups attended by a total of 80 sets of parents and babies. This
chapter is the product of a constant process of feedback from
participants, my co-facilitators and my reflections in supervision.

AIMS

My aim for groups is to increase parental **sensitive caregiving**,
empathy and mind-mindedness, wondering what may be going on for
baby (Meins *et al.* 2011). Whenever possible I work with a co-facilitator
using the format of watching and filming the babies and parents,
and showing the group 'better than usual' moments of interaction
(Kennedy, Landor and Todd 2011). I want to encourage reverie and
reflection on the babies, their relationships to their parents and to

each other. In this way I hope that parents can begin to focus on real-time interactions and relationships rather than their perception being clouded by images of past negative relationships (Baradon *et al*. 2005). To support this shift from 'ghosts' to 'angels' (Lieberman 2007), I aim to create a friendly **mirroring** experience in the group for both babies and for parents.

BACKGROUND

My enthusiasm for parent–baby groups and for the powerful impact of positive images prompted me to experiment with combining the two. I found that the overall impact of a curious and sympathetic Watch, Wait and Wonder stance (Cohen *et al*. 1999; see Glossary) in a group of parents and babies and the prompts of benign visual images showing successful interactions, time and again created situations that were moving, profound and helped some parents to engage in thoughtful reflections. Even parents who struggled to use words and could not engage in conversations about the quality of their past significant relationships (Lieberman 2007) were able to experience the attunement created in the groups, and responded well to seeing themselves in positive visual images. They also benefitted from the comments of other parents; over the course of three to six months, most group participants showed a noticeable shift, and became more friendly, sensitive and attuned towards their babies. Professionals in the children's centre where the group took place also noticed the positive impact of the group on the women and babies.

THEORETICAL FRAMEWORKS

BODY-BASED EMPATHY

Our first experience of understanding another is always visceral and body-based. This is how babies learn about the world and how they communicate with their carers, and is also known as implicit intersubjectivity (Trevarthen 2009). **Kinaesthetic empathy** and embodied **mentalization** (feeling with your body what may be going on inside the other) are the initial steps most parents employ to form attuned relationships (Shai and Belsky 2011) as they try to understand their baby, and this is also what group facilitators do as they aim to be 'appropriately responsive' to all group participants (parents and babies).

Schore and Schore (1999) say that 'nonverbal affect-laden primary process communication is implicit and represents the attachment dynamic. The polyvagal theory (Porges 2011) supports this argument. Parent-baby groups are a coming together of many primitive and non-verbal intentions and events, as well as verbal interactions which are all taking place at the same time.

ANALYTIC CONCEPTS

Ideas emerging from my supervision groups included Bion's (1968) concept of the group as a container, which describes the function of the group as a space where parents could feel safe to express difficulties. The impact of the 'outer container', in my case the children's centre, was crucial, as it provided the physical space and the welcoming environment that are instrumental in recruiting and retaining group participants as well as sharing child protection concerns (see also Chapter 4). A further helpful concept was Foulkes's idea of the group as a matrix, which moves from dependence on the leader towards more independence, self-reliance, and mutual understanding and nurture (Foulkes 1984; Happy & Well 2014; James 2016).

INTERACTION OF NEURO-PHYSICAL AND
EMOTIONAL STATES BETWEEN PEOPLE

A distressed baby will activate distress in all of us; the sound of a crying baby will make us feel uncomfortable. **Polyvagal contagion** is our unconscious reaction to the state of excitement in another person. Our nervous system responds to others' nervous systems (Porges 2011). There is a link between our eyes, reacting to another's facial expressions, our gut hormones involving digestion, and stress or relaxation. Research on mirror neurons further supports this hypothesis (Bråten 2007). A neuro-physiological framework helps us to think about the flow of emotional states between people (Siegel 2009). Everyone in baby groups works hard to keep the babies settled and calm. A well-functioning mother baby group is a 'working group', a concept coined by Bion (1968) meaning 'a co-operating entity for mutual support'. A group such as this will activate the mammalian vagus of everyone present, which is linked to comforting, soothing and feeding. The group therefore generates enough of a benign atmosphere to switch on the care-taking system, to soothe and be soothed. Everyone in the room is affected. Babies are great levellers; their physical and emotional needs are immediate. They are the focus for all of us in a group as we try to manage the constant flux of 'being with'.

CONTEXT

The vignettes described in this chapter took place in groups I ran at different children's centres with families from diverse socio-economic backgrounds. They included two sets of twins and three fathers among the parents. On average there were six to seven dyads per group. The babies' ages ranged from 6 to 16 months. Most families were referred by health visitors, midwives, the children's centre family and outreach workers, and some self-referred.

The groups were run weekly for one hour, mainly during term time, with some parents joining or leaving at half-term break, and some staying in the group for two terms (up to eight months maximum). All parents were first seen individually with their baby and encouraged to tell the story of their pregnancy and birth, as well as what it was like in the early weeks and months of becoming parents. I always asked what other sources of support were current in a family's life.

THE FORMAT

Initially I greeted and welcomed all arrivals, noticing any changes and new developmental achievements. I supported parents and babies to settle in the circle prepared on the floor (floor covers, toys for the babies and cushions for parents to sit on). We sang the hello song, acknowledging each individual participant, parents and babies, and followed up on events from the previous week.

This was followed by showing short video clips or stills from the last session of *better than usual* moments (Kennedy *et al.* 2011). I invited comments on the images and aimed to relate them back to the babies in the room. Then we practised watching the babies for about five minutes with, if possible, one facilitator filming while the other was watching the group actively. The instructions to the parents were to watch the babies and notice their initiatives, as well as their own internal response, but not to start anything new. It was important to say this clearly and to explain that it did not mean not to respond at all (*which was sometimes how parents could hear what was said*), but to be receptive and responsive, whilst giving space, and most importantly to give completely undivided attention to the babies.

Afterwards we reflected on the experience. I often asked whether the time watching felt long or short, as this gave a good indication of how engrossed a parent could be. The conversation followed the events and themes arising from the group. We finished the session with the goodbye song, which created, via a simple rhythm, a sense of togetherness before saying goodbye.

AN INITIAL SESSION

The following group had four dyads (nine participants, including the facilitator). Thea, an anxious professional, had initially confessed that she did not enjoy Leo, her five-month-old baby: 'He was overly active and never content.' Roberta, a white-collar worker, was surprised by the intensity of her feelings for her baby Frances, aged 11 months, who was extremely mobile and curious. Roberta said she felt both delight and sadness at noticing the passing of this precious time. Maria, of non-British origin, had suffered from postnatal depression with her first child and felt worried and obsessed by lack of sleep. Her son Elias could not yet sit and she was concerned about his development. Karen, a single mother, was a shy young woman who had come to this town to get away from an abusive home environment. The father of her baby did not live with her, and was at times threatening. She wanted her son Chris to be independent and social, 'not like myself'.

In the first session we watched twice for five minutes each time, filming once. The instructions were to pay attention to baby and follow her/his cues. The babies were intensely curious of each other.

PARENTS' REFLECTIONS AFTER WATCHING THE BABIES

Roberta noticed she felt anxious that her daughter Frances might do something to others and she would be held responsible. This developed into a theme and parents shared that they all worried about how their toddler's behaviour might reflect badly on them. They expressed concerns that their baby might hurt another. They also wondered if they could be spontaneous, as they were watching and being watched by the camera, and by implication, myself the facilitator. Thea realized how hard it was to let her son be, and how surprised she was that he was so content during the five minutes' watching. Karen responded saying that she too had felt like that in the past. Maria said it was a relief to just sit back and watch.

MY REFLECTION

Looking at the footage after the session I was struck by how much all mothers looked out for *all* the babies. I had originally thought that the parent-baby dyads would be centre stage, but it was the multiple interactions between babies and babies, and babies and all the other adults, which dominated the events in this group.

LOOKING AND FEELING – THE IMPACT OF FILMING

Anna, aged 25, had been identified as vulnerable. She had cared for her disabled mother and four siblings from early age, left home at 14, and moved in with her partner's family. She struggled to follow her daughter Rosie's initiatives. I showed her a still of when she followed Rosie's gaze towards a toy. Her first reaction was, 'I must lose weight!'

This is not an unusual response. When we look at a photo we always look at ourselves first. It is fascinating to see oneself from the outside. Often we just see our faults. When questioned if her toddler also thought the same, Anna replied, 'Oh no, she just sees mummy.' In this exchange there was already an expression of how mother felt about herself on the inside, and at the same time a shift in her thinking, as she recognized that her daughter will have a different perception to her.

Karen, looking at images of herself and her baby from a prior session, exclaimed, 'Oh I'm wearing the same dress as last week, you must think I never change my clothes!' This comment gave rise to a conversation that as new mothers we sometimes are so focused on the babies that we forget to look after ourselves. It also hinted at a fear of being judged negatively by others. This did not happen. In the following sessions Karen was more attentive, and could observe how her baby Chris was curious about the other babies.

SHARED PLEASURE

Britta was cautious and afraid her nine-month-old daughter Rae would get hurt. Initially we could not get a clip of longer than 15 seconds before Britta interfered and moved Rae to 'safety'. I showed her a clip of her looking adoringly at her toddler, with Rae returning the gaze. When Britta saw this moment of attunement, she was delighted. On a second viewing Britta noticed how she gently bounced in the same rhythm as her daughter. We all shared Britta's pleasure and baby Rae laughed with a big smile in response to her mother's delight. Britta then said to her, 'You love your baby watching!'

In my supervision group we recounted this moment, but wondered if the mother ascribed the pleasure to the baby when she was actually talking about herself. Over time Britta's confidence increased and she allowed her daughter more freedom to explore.

When I show parents positive images of themselves, it is as if this switches on the caregiving, loving system. This is amplified by experiencing other parents and babies enjoying their own and others babies. It is as if the pleasure principle is allowed and encouraged in an atmosphere of warmth, acceptance and curiosity. This then enables parents to give their babies more space without the need to interfere.

SOME CHALLENGES FOR THE GROUP FACILITATOR

I notice that as my confidence grows I have become more effective at explaining the purpose and benefit of filming to parents. I tend to acknowledge that initially it is normal to be a little apprehensive. It is extremely important to give a parent space to comment on how they feel about looking at themselves, especially when they see themselves for the first time on film. Once they experience the pleasure of seeing themselves with their baby at good moments, they tend to be keen to continue this process.

There have been practical considerations. For instance, what should I do when I had a clip showing great attunement, but the parent missed the following session? Should I re-edit, to add it to the next film I would show the following week, or leave it for the very end of the group when every parent received a copy of the best moments to take home? There are no fixed answers, but I often tend to add the best moments to the following edit, as I always try to have something to show to each dyad.

At first I had a tendency to film too much, which became rather time-consuming, to watch, micro-analyse and edit. Over time I learned to edit whilst filming and became more confident to know that I had managed to capture a good enough moment to show.

One big challenge is when a baby has an 'off' day and grizzles throughout the watching part of the session. This could sometimes be baby's way of expressing a parent's anxiety, or it could be that baby is just tired, hungry or unwell. How to manage these moments is at the heart of the Baby Watching groups, as parents may feel exposed and need support to find their own way of coping. From a filming perspective, it is impossible to use footage that has a voice track of an unhappy baby, as this would raise stress hormones in the viewer and so increase discomfort even more, which would be counterproductive. I therefore never knowingly show unhappy moments, unless they are resolved quickly. If no other footage can be found, I turn off the sound or just use stills.

I will make sure I capture good moments with *each* participating dyad. This depends on positioning and light, where the parent sits in the circle, how far the baby moves away from the parent, how comfortable the facilitator is in moving around whilst filming, or even requesting parents to shift a bit in the circle to fit into the camera frame.

MANAGING THE PRESENT MOMENT

Parent and baby groups are never static, but in constant flux, as babies' needs are urgent, and their interests uninhibited. The parents' task is always to manage their babies and regulate their excitement, to respond appropriately to the constantly changing rhythms and flow of the unexpected; how much space to give, and when to intervene, verbally or non-verbally, was an ongoing dilemma, and a common theme.

Rosa was just learning to balance. She crawled towards the door of the room and pulled herself up with great concentration. Des, who was the same age, but much bigger, approached her. He also wanted to stand up, and he used Rosa to support himself. There was a moment when both were balancing precariously, then they started to sway and eventually toppled over. All the adults in the group were watching, and exclaimed as one when the pair fell. Quickly both toddlers crawled back to their mummies, not sure if they should be upset, and the parents managed to reassure them. Anna then talked proudly about how Rosa had just learned to stand up, and Des's mother said she was concerned he may hurt Rosa. I commented on the excitement that had gripped us all.

REFLECTION

When we watched this exchange the following week on film, Anna said how amazed she was, as in her memory the event seemed much longer than when it actually happened. This was an interesting comment, as it showed how when we are totally focused our perception of time can change. Ultimately I want to support parents to learn to be present and attentive in the moment, rather than be preoccupied with past or future events. I find that when parents become more trusting of themselves and their babies, they are able to relax and experience what can also be described as 'flow', 'when you are so completely absorbed by an activity that nothing else seems to matter' (Buchanan and Csikszentmihalyi 1991).

One unintended consequence of filming is that it gives me an opportunity to observe myself and micro-analyse my interactions with group participants. One such snapshot showed baby Ezra marvelling with excitement at his reflection in a shiny disc. I exchanged a glance with his mother, confirming non-verbally that I had seen what she had noticed. Her smile grew. Within a fraction of a second my expression changed as I noticed that baby Helen was starting to grumble. Then I exchanged glances with baby Sybil, who watched the shiny disc, and my eyebrows shot up in a classic marked mirroring expression (exaggerated facial expressions, to empathize with babies, an amplification of their feeling state), joining in her surprise and pleasure, and back again with a concerned look to my co-facilitator and Helen's mother, who eventually picked Helen up to comfort her. All these expressions took place in less than a minute.

I realized then how much my face works, as I relate to all babies and adults in the room, my attention shifting – alert to the many communications and feelings in the group. Equally, even though I am quite tall, I noticed that I grow and shrink in response to whom I am communicating with. This would also affect where and how I positioned myself in the circle, and whom I chose to sit next to.

Ilana, aged 23, had been abandoned by her family to traffickers. She managed to escape, and was lucky to receive housing and support in this country. She was very loving to Katarina, her 11-month-old toddler, but extremely protective and tended to restrict her movements. Equally she was insistent that Katarina 'does not like groups'. I made a conscious effort to sit next to her, as I felt my physical proximity did benefit this dyad. It was the little shifts of posture and my admiring gaze that I think contributed to helping Ilana feel safe, so that after a few sessions she could exclaim, 'Look at Katarina, she learned to walk last week, did you film that?'

In supervision we reflected on how I as the facilitator function like a conductor, by moving my attention and attuning, with my body, with vocalization and with words, to help contain and to make sense of constantly shifting events. Using embodied mentalization and receiving babies and parents at great speed was at the heart of this process (Shai and Belsky 2011).

Baby Watching groups involve many possible combinations of mirroring, between parent and baby, baby and other adults, baby and other babies, parents and other parents, and all with the facilitators (Celebi 2014; James 2016). This experience is amplified by the better than usual visual images I show parents.

Seeing themselves at moments of attunement gives parents a sense of an alternative hopeful narrative, which paradoxically often frees them to talk about challenges and the times when they are struggling. The benign comments from others help parents to internalize more positive aspects of themselves, and this gives them courage to be open in the group (Celebi 2014).

DEVELOPMENTS IN THE GROUPS

I have discovered that it is crucial to show images of attunement of parents with their baby from the start, as this sets the expectations for the group. We can all admire and enjoy together these good moments. I have noticed a shift from parents initially only looking at themselves, to starting to focus on their baby and finally on babies' interactions with others.

The group's focus also shifted from initial concerns, such as 'will my baby hurt or get hurt?', to shared delight in seeing the babies interact, and looking out for each baby's safety, pondering on similarities and differences, and reflecting on their parenting experiences.

Over time I have had more opportunities to film then show clips of the group as a whole, rather than dyads only. This is my visual commentary on the group's process. The group thus becomes a friendly multi-mirror, and group participants' comments are amplified by the *better than usual* visual images – encouraging mentalization, reflecting on babies, their intentions and feelings.

The stimulating group environment also activates the mirror neurons and, I assume, lights up the caregiving brain circuits (Panksepp and Biven 2007). This process enhances the pleasant experience of all group participants. We feel loving and loved, and want to look after the babies and each other.

CONCLUSION

The use of technology in the groups together with a Watch, Wait and Wonder stance of non-judgemental curiosity helps to enhance the benign mirroring experience of all participants, parents, babies and facilitators. It seems to increase the ability of parents to reflect on their present relationship with their babies. Starting with moments of strength, showing attunement, paradoxically frees parents to also share some of the negative internal narratives. They notice possible contradictions between their assumptions and the visual evidence to the contrary, which is enhanced by the friendly feedback from other group participants. This combination creates conditions for change, a heightened sensitivity and understanding of babies' real (not imagined) needs.

Finally I would like to reiterate that this chapter describes work in progress and has not covered all the angles that may occur and that one can possibly think of. My hope is, however, that sharing my experiences will encourage others to continue adjusting and developing this way of working in groups and therefore further nurture and grow parents' love and sensitivity towards their babies.

REFERENCES

Baradon, T., with Broughton, C., Gibbs, I., James, J., Joyce, A. and Woodhead, J. of the Parent-Infant Project at the Anna Freud Centre (2005) *The Practice of Psychoanalytic Parent-Infant Psychotherapy: Claiming the Baby.* New York: Taylor & Francis.

Bion, W.R. (1968) *Experiences in Groups, and Other Papers.* London: Tavistock.

Bråten, S. (ed.) (2007) *On Being Moved: From Mirror Neurons to Empathy.* Amsterdam: John Benjamins.

Buchanan, R. and Csikszentmihalyi, M. (1991) 'Flow: the psychology of optimal experience.' *Design Issues 8*, 1, 80.

Celebi, M. (2014) 'Baby watching: facilitating parent-infant interaction groups.' *Journal of Health Visiting 2*, 7, 362–367.

Cohen, N.J., Muir, E., Lojkasek, M., Muir, R., Parker, C.J., Barwick, M. and Brown, M. (1999) 'Watch, wait, and wonder: testing the effectiveness of a new approach to mother-infant psychotherapy.' *Infant Mental Health Journal 20*, 4, 429–451.

Foulkes, S.H. (1984) *Therapeutic Group Analysis.* London: Maresfield Reprints.

Happy & Well (2014) *Living in Flow – The Secret of Happiness with Mihaly Csikszentmihalyi at Happiness & Its Causes 2014.* Available at: https://youtu.be/TzPky5Xe1-s (Accessed: 6 December 2016).

James, J. (2016) 'Parent-Infant Psychotherapy in Groups.' In T. Baradon with M. Biseo, C. Broughton, J. James and A. Joyce *The Practice of Psychoanalytic Parent-Infant Psychotherapy: Claiming the Baby.* 2nd edn. London: Routledge.

Kennedy, H., Landor, M. and Todd, L. (eds) (2011) *Video Interaction Guidance: A Relationship-Based Intervention to Promote Attunement, Empathy and Wellbeing.* Philadelphia: Jessica Kingsley Publishers.

Lieberman, A.F. (2007) 'Ghosts and angels: intergenerational patterns in the transmission and treatment of the traumatic sequelae of domestic violence.' *Infant Mental Health Journal 28*, 4, 422–439.

Meins, E., Fernyhough, C., Arnott, B., Turner, M. and Leekam, S.R. (2011) 'Mother-versus infant-centered correlates of maternal mind-mindedness in the first year of life.' *Infancy 16*, 2, 137–165.

Panksepp, J. and Biven, L. (2007) *The Archaeology of Mind: Neuroevolutionary Origins of Human Emotions.* New York: W.W. Norton.

Porges, S.W. (2011) *The Polyvagal Theory: Neurophysiological Foundations of Emotions, Attachment, Communication, and Self-Regulation.* New York: W.W. Norton.

Schore, A.N. and Schore, S. (1999) *Affect Regulation and the Origin of the Self: The Neurobiology of Emotional Development.* Hillsdale, NJ: Lawrence Erlbaum Associates.

Shai, D. and Belsky, J. (2011) 'Parental embodied mentalizing: let's be explicit about what we mean by implicit.' *Child Development Perspectives 5*, 3, 187–188.

Siegel, D.J. (2009) 'Mindful awareness, mindsight, and neural integration.' *The Humanistic Psychologist 37*, 2, 137–158.

Trevarthen, C. (2009) 'Embodied human intersubjectivity: imaginative agency, to share meaning.' *Cognitive Semiotics 4*, 1, 6–56.

GROUPS FOR PARENTS AND BABIES NEEDING EXTRA SUPPORT

CHAPTER 8

The Ordinary Devoted Group

Developing a Parent and Baby Psychotherapy Group

Caryn Onions

This chapter describes the setting up and development of a therapeutic parent and baby group. Vignettes from group sessions are used to highlight areas of interest.

WINNICOTT'S 'ORDINARY DEVOTED MOTHER'

In 1966 Winnicott, the well-known paediatrician and psychoanalyst, gave a talk to the Nursery School Association entitled 'The Ordinary Devoted Mother' (Winnicott 1988). I have adapted the title of Winnicott's talk for this chapter as I feel it reflects my experience of co-running a parent-baby psychotherapy group. We were doing an ordinary thing: sitting, talking about the parents' experiences of being new mothers and playing with women and their babies, yet at the same time it felt like an extraordinary experience.

Winnicott did not use the word 'devoted' in a sentimental way, even though he is sometimes criticized for this, but I believe what he meant was the way the mother will offer, dedicate and apply herself to her baby. My co-worker Geraldine Stemp and I felt this is what we did. We offered, applied and dedicated ourselves not only to the idea of the group, but also to each other. It was our first time of working together, and our attachment to each other and the group developed in parallel.

WHY A PARENT-BABY PSYCHOTHERAPY GROUP?

I ran this group whilst working for the Oxford Parent Infant Project (OXPIP), a parent-baby psychotherapy service within the voluntary sector. I had previously run several groups for mothers of sexually abused children in another work setting and was fascinated by how a safe, well-run group can help people share and discover their feelings. The process of being in a group seemed to help people put voice to, and uncover, shared views in ways that were different to individual work with parents, and so I wanted to see what it would be like to have mothers and babies together in the same group. I was influenced by group analytic principles (Foulkes 1983) and the work of Paul and Thomson-salo (1997). Both of these approaches assume that the 'analysis' of the individual within the context of a group is a therapeutically sound approach.

BABIES AS GROUP MEMBERS

I wanted to explore the possibility of babies having a place as group members in their own right, alongside their mothers sharing their difficulties and concerns with other mother-baby pairs. The aim was that therapy could progress through observation and discussion of the babies' behaviour; by thinking about what was happening with the mothers in the group. At the beginning of this project Geraldine and I started regular supervision with a group analyst to help us think about how to work as co-therapists, how to model being a thinking parental couple, as well as how to understand what took place in the group.

ASSESSING MOTHERS

The group was advertised to all the agencies that referred to our service. At assessment we met each mother two to three times, giving them the opportunity to tell their story to one of us. What each mother told us in their assessment was confidential and several issues discussed during the assessments never came to light in the group, for instance childhood experiences of neglect or abuse, but each mother knew that one of us held that information in our mind. We explained how the group would be run and discussed their and our commitment to it.

GROUP MEMBERSHIP

Initially we wanted to run an ongoing slow open group (where new mothers could join established group members) for between five and six mother baby dyads, that is, up to 12 members. Owing to organizational and funding reasons, however, the group had a fixed membership of 5 mothers with their babies and lasted for 18 months. The babies were aged two to three months when they joined. We hoped that the earlier we brought the babies into a group, the sooner there would be an opportunity to help strengthen their mothers' capacity to respond to and recognize their baby's cues within the holding therapeutic environment of the group.

THE MOTHERS

None of the women who attended had previous experience of long-term therapy. They came from different socio-economic and ethnic backgrounds, and had quite different educational experiences. For two it was their first child. They were all in an ongoing relationship with their baby's father; however, they shared profound feelings of self-doubt and low self-esteem about mothering their child, and each one had recently seen her GP for depression and anxiety. A second common feature was relationship difficulties stemming from various childhood experiences. Becoming a mother had seriously affected their emotional wellbeing and they were struggling to manage day-to-day living.

WHAT IS DIFFERENT ABOUT A PSYCHOTHERAPY GROUP?

Our group was based on group analytic principles and as such was not a mother and baby group, nor an advice or drop-in group. There was no tea or coffee, and no social chatting. Yet it was a warm and friendly environment, but we were serious about its purpose. It ran for an hour and a half, and we always started and finished on time. The importance of confidentiality was stressed along with the possible complications for the mothers of meeting outside the group. These *rules* were adhered to, to ensure the emotional safety of everyone.

VENUE AND ROOM

The group was held in the same room, at the same time each week, in a local health centre. Each adult sat on a floor cushion and in the centre we put a large piece of quilted fabric between us all. Each baby had their own mat. Geraldine and I sat opposite each other so we could make eye contact and see each other easily, although no one was fixed to any set position. We provided the same box of toys each week. There was a small weekly charge and the attendance rate was approximately 80 per cent.

SETTLING IN – GETTING TO KNOW EACH OTHER

In the beginning phase of the group the mothers and babies arrived at varying times, with one mother arriving consistently late for the first term. We wondered with the group what arriving late could mean, and the mothers replied quickly saying they were disappointed that we did not meet more often and that once a week did not feel enough. The mother who arrived late laughed at the irony of *wanting more but getting less*. It was interesting how this developed into a theme that they all shared, how they could want one thing but actually end up doing the opposite. This was repeated throughout the group and was evident especially when they talked about family relationships and how they felt they did what everyone else wanted them to do. During the course of the group they all worked hard to try and change their tendency to conform and this reduced their feelings of resentment.

STARTING TO SHARE WORRIES

This is an excerpt from session three. It shows how quickly the group started working even though at this stage they knew very little about each other.

Emily was sitting cross-legged with baby Ed held very close, breastfeeding. He appeared physically relaxed. Emily then said with some trepidation and anxiety, 'When I'm upset and feeding him I'm a bit scared that I'm poisoning him with it.' Others seemed to understand her concerns, and a short while later Marie said tearfully, 'I worry about that too with Chloe.' Steph then shared a very different concern saying, 'I walked out of a shop on my own the other day as I forgot I had Tom.'

The mothers realized early on that we could tolerate them talking about very powerful feelings, and that this would be understood by everyone in the group. In this example, Emily was beginning to describe how unsure she was about her nurturing capacities: would her mind contaminate her milk and would this affect Ed? She was starting to let us know how concerned she was that her own distressing thoughts and feelings might get right inside her baby. Marie strongly identified with Emily's dilemma and painfully recalled how her own mother struggled when she was young, and how for as long as she could remember Marie felt it was her job to make her mother feel better. She was terrified that she too was already repeating this with Chloe. Steph was facing a different set of problems, when in the early days she would make light of the fact that Tom was not in her mind at all.

HELPING MOTHERS FIND THE ANSWERS

The mothers were faced with the common dilemma for new parents of how to nurture their baby whilst at the same time grappling with their own feelings of childhood, which were flooding back, and sometimes quite intrusively. As facilitators of the group, Geraldine and I did not see our role as giving advice, but instead as helping the mothers make links between the things they were feeling, saying and doing in order to increase their understanding about themselves as new mothers.

Clinically I believe that my role as a child psychotherapist is to develop the capacity of parents to understand themselves in relation to their child, not to offer practical suggestions about parenting and child rearing. During the first few months of the group we had to firmly resist requests for advice and at times we felt as if we were withholding the right answer or the magical solution to the mothers' problems. It is possible that their strong desire for advice reflected their yearning for a trusted older maternal figure.

WEANING AND SEPARATION

The middle phase of the group coincided with the babies reaching a similar stage where weaning and separation were key developmental tasks. For anxious mothers who have found it difficult to bond with their babies, this can be a difficult time.

Steph was in her mid-thirties and whilst she had not completely concealed the pregnancy with Tom, she did not talk about it. Her work colleagues were speechless when she announced that she was going on maternity leave, having had no idea that she was pregnant. It seemed as if she had not even managed to tell herself that she was having a baby. During the first few months of the group we began to understand just how *cut off* Steph had been from her body and all its changes, and from any pregnant thoughts in her mind.

BABIES GROWING UP

Five months into the group, however, Steph said she was becoming 'obsessed' with Tom and on one day when feeling particularly low she said to him, 'You don't give any of your smiles to me any more.' It was as if she felt that when he smiled at someone else it was a rejection of her, which she felt acutely. One session when he slept most of the time, she said tearfully that she felt lost and abandoned in the group when he was asleep. She struggled with very powerful feelings of guilt for the mixed emotions she had felt about the pregnancy. It seemed as if five months into the group when Tom was eight months old, she had finally caught up with the fact that she was a mother and that she had a baby. Her infatuation with him was like a love affair and she could not bear it if he paid attention to someone else. It was as if she had to cram in all her new-found loving, maternally preoccupied feelings before he got too old and toddled off by himself.

The session before the Easter break started off with the mothers reviewing the past seven months. Unusually Steph had dressed Tom, now 10 months old, in a baby-gro, which looked quite incongruous, as he was big now, and she generally tended to dress him in older-looking clothes such as jeans and a sweatshirt. It made more sense, however, once she said that she now thought that she had not been emotionally ready for a baby; how it had been such a shock that she pretended it was not happening. Whilst talking to the group, one minute she was holding Tom by his fingers encouraging him to walk, and a few minutes later was giving him a breastfeed and joking to us that her milk was like 'lager on tap'. Later, when she was talking about her struggle to stop breastfeeding and put him in his own bed, she said, 'He's got to wean me off. It's me who's holding him back!'

REFLECTION

This vignette shows how Steph felt safe enough in the group to explore her contradictory feelings. Tom was starting to separate from his mother, pulling to standing and enjoying the experience of his new-found bodily strength. Yet, Steph dressed him as a much younger baby, whilst toying with the idea of providing him with 'lager on tap'. She was struggling to think about him growing up when she had only just realized that he had been born. This led her to feel guilty and sad that she had missed so much, but it did help her to understand why she had ended up in the group and to be pleased that she was doing something positive to help them both.

The babies' inevitable development forced the mothers to think about the future. They talked about their bodies returning to *normal*, their periods restarting and a desire to want their bodies back without too much guilt. When talking about her relationship with her husband, Emily said, 'I'm not so worried about being unfaithful to Ed [her son] now if we have sex.' Here Emily felt unfaithful to her son when she made love to her husband, which suggests the passionate and intense preoccupation that motherhood can bring. It is probably also no coincidence that the developmental stage of the baby sitting or standing up and looking at their parents has important psychological effects on the mother herself, and the parental couple.

USING THE BABIES TO UNDERSTAND THE MOTHERS' FEELING

Understanding the dynamics of the group and how to use that in the group was sometimes a challenge. We began to notice a real difference in the quality of how the mothers related and spoke to each other, and how they used us as facilitators. They tried to help each other think and asked each other for help. The following excerpts are a good example of the therapeutic potential of groups, where normal sibling rivalry can turn into concern for each other.

WORKING WITH THE INDIVIDUAL IN THE GROUP

This vignette focuses on Stella and Billy. Stella went through periods of arriving very late. She would sometimes make dramatic and shocking statements when she arrived, or sit and cry silently. Her behaviour often had the effect of diverting the attention to her and away from the issue being discussed in the group. This often left Geraldine and me with strong feelings of resentment and irritation. We used supervision to help us work out what may be going on for Stella and in the group as a whole and how to respond, and this enabled us to become more empathetic towards Stella.

BABIES FASCINATED BY EACH OTHER DEVELOPED A GAME

On one occasion Stella and Billy arrived 45 minutes late. Stella did not give any reason and baby Billy went on to have a great time with baby Chloe. Over the past few weeks, these two children had developed a game of sucking and biting each other on the head, and the mothers had previously commented that there seemed to be some mutual attraction between the two of them. Chloe, who had fine wispy blonde hair, seemed spellbound by Billy's dark curls, which she would grab with both hands, and in return, he seemed fascinated by her golden locks.

LINKING WHAT IS SAID ABOUT EVENTS OUTSIDE THE GROUP TO EVENTS HAPPENING IN THE GROUP

After a while Stella told the group that she had recently taken part in some research on attachment, which involved being videoed, and that the researcher had given her positive feedback, telling her that Billy had a secure attachment to her. She recounted how she had told her husband, and how she thought he had been jealous that Stella had been praised for her parenting. I felt that she was telling the group that she was a good mother, it had been proved by the video, and that the researcher was better than us as she had told Stella something we were not saying.

BABY SEEKING COMFORT

During this conversation, Billy and Chloe continued their sucking, biting game and we did not see exactly what happened, but Billy started crying and seemed to almost collapse on the lower part of my legs. I leant forward, putting my hands either side of his arms and shoulders, to give him some comfort. He was shaking and making a noise, which was not quite a cry but what in the group we all referred to as 'trilling', and in the past he had done it when he seemed frustrated or overwhelmed by something. I looked to Stella, expecting her to move towards him, but she just looked and made a sort of laugh at Billy and made no move towards us. Stella was encouraging me to cuddle him for what seemed ages, but it was probably only a few seconds. I could not understand why she did not come and get him and I felt irritated with her. As I could see she was not going to take him, I knelt up and leant over towards the middle of the mat with Billy in my arms; eventually she took him, and he calmed quickly.

PARENTS' ATTENDANCE PATTERNS AS UNCONSCIOUS RESPONSE TO EVENTS AND FEELINGS EXPRESSED

The next week three mothers called to say they could not attend and Geraldine and I wondered if it had something to do with this event. Steph was 10 minutes late and Stella 25 minutes late. Stella said that after the group last week they had spoken together outside about my reaction and they had decided that my reluctance to cuddle Billy was probably something to do with the boundaries of the group. Stella asked me why I looked uncomfortable comforting Billy, and I said that at that point when Billy dropped onto my legs, she was talking about her husband feeling jealous and not such a good parent as her. She said she did not remember saying that about her husband; she had no recollection at all.

RELATIONSHIP BETWEEN A MOTHER AND FACILITATOR

Steph helpfully said that she did not like it if someone else comforted baby Tom. She was pleased now to think that Tom wanted to be comforted by her, whereas she used to find it overwhelming when he was younger. Stella disagreed and said she was pleased that Billy could go to others. As the conversation progressed, I said to Stella that I had the sense that she might be feeling rejected by me not comforting Billy. She initially disagreed but after a while began to think this was probably right, and together we worked out that she took my reaction as evidence that she was not wanted or liked, rather than seeing me as someone who wanted to support her parenting and bring her and Billy together. She agreed that I had not been like the researcher who complimented her; in fact, she turned me into the opposite, and later likened me to Cruella de Vil.

I had felt put in an impossible position by Stella and this mirrored the situations that we would regularly hear about in her life. I had not felt Billy wanted me to cuddle him and there seemed to have been a mismatch between what we observed and what Stella thought was happening. I said I thought Billy was on my legs because I was the nearest person to him, but that he had not cuddled into me, and my presence had not stopped his distress.

BABIES ENACTING A MOTHER'S UNCONSCIOUS FEELINGS

The biting, sucking game did have an aggressive, attacking quality, much like the comments and behaviours that Stella could sometimes drop into the group, and in supervision we wondered if Billy was enacting something for his mother

A few weeks earlier Billy had seemed frightened by Tom, as Tom was going through a phase of screeching, often directed at Billy. Billy would 'trill', shake his arms and seem unable to move or crawl away, he was almost frozen or dissociated. At these times Stella was always somewhat slow, slightly mocking and reluctant to comfort him, and on reflection, given her childhood history of abuse and domestic violence, we wondered whether some of her early experiences were being re-enacted in the group. It appeared difficult for the mothers to say anything to Stella about her lateness and the things she said, even though Geraldine and I made lots of comments and felt we gave plenty of opportunities for someone to say something. We now wondered whether the sessions where Tom frightened Billy might have been an enactment of his mother's or the adults' annoyance with Stella.

How to address these issues effectively in a group setting was a challenge and at times we struggled to contain Stella and to pull these things into the group context in order to make parallel links with other members in the group. The overt level of disagreement and conflict between the mothers and us was minimal. Whenever there were differences of opinion, we usually tried to find a common understanding. Perhaps had we been able to talk about how the children's behaviour might have mirrored the interpersonal feelings between the mothers, then we may have been able to help them differently. Closely observing and taking seriously what the babies were doing certainly helped my understanding of the dynamics in the group.

ENDING THOUGHTS

Being with mothers and babies in a group analytic setting is therapeutically powerful. Each parent-baby relationship is on view for all to see, and working in the *here and now* with what we observed happening between mother and baby was a potent tool for change. At the start the mothers were simultaneously grappling with differing feelings of intimacy and distance towards their babies. Over many months, however, their ability to share with the group these opposite positions towards their babies gradually helped them arrive at a more comfortable position, something less extreme and more tolerable.

The mothers could be compassionate to each other's dilemmas, but the support they got from the group was much more than a *propping up*. In fact, they were able to say things to each other that Geraldine and I would have found difficult in our role as facilitators. Maintaining the boundaries of the group helped them feel safe enough to share and explore extremely intimate and distressing thoughts and feelings: one mother talked about being raped in her early twenties and the group helped her decide to go for counselling, whilst another talked about episodes of self-harm during her teens.

THE LAST GROUP

During the last group the toddlers (all now over 20 months old) slept until the last two minutes of the session. This had never happened before. It was not their usual naptime, and it was odd for them to arrive asleep and to not be woken by the noises in the group. The mothers were as surprised by this as we were. We all thought there was something powerful being conveyed to us about the group ending. Steph told us that Tom had woken crying for several nights running saying, 'Wishy stopped, wishy stopped', 'wishy' being his name for the washing machine. She told us that he loved the washing machine and was fascinated by it. Together we wondered if he was also showing his and their sadness that the group was ending. As facilitators, we also felt the sadness as our original plan had been for the group to become an ongoing resource for mothers assessed as needing long-term therapy. We felt the group had stopped prematurely, because of lack of funding, and so were disappointed that this was not going to happen.

The group members had shown their commitment by attending for 18 months. They attended during a time when it is often difficult for new mothers with small babies regularly to get out of the house.

WHY GROUPS?

I think that where possible this type of intervention should be the preferred option if a mother and baby need longer-term psychotherapy. This is not to say that individual work is not helpful, but in a group setting mothers learn so much from listening to and observing each other. The experience of being in a group with other mothers greatly reduces common feelings of guilt and shame, especially nowadays when mothers are bombarded with images of happy women and their families. Being with her baby also brings to life a mother's own attachment pattern and past narratives. This means that feelings and experiences can sometimes be accessed more quickly in a group than during individual work. This is an area with huge potential for further research.

Culturally, we have lost the experience of sharing life-changing transitions such as having a baby. Being in a group and hearing other mothers talk can help women to see their situation through a different lens.

Groups can be difficult to get started. This has to be taken into account in the planning stage and when raising funds. Hence, the support and backing of the decision makers in an organization is crucial. Groups are affected by the organizational climate and funding uncertainties. Once established, however, a slow open group where new members join along the way can be a highly effective treatment.

The title of this chapter, 'The Ordinary Devoted Group', refers to the ideas we had when the group began: a regular, shared space where mothers could talk about and share their feelings about a very ordinary, yet extraordinary thing, their relationship with their baby. Winnicott had the ability to understand the complexities of becoming a mother, and the developing relationship with her baby, and this group is an example of how to provide that opportunity to mothers.

REFERENCES

Foulkes, S.H. (1983) *Introduction to Group Analytic Psychotherapy: Studies in the Social Integration of Individuals and Groups*. London: Karnac Books.

Paul, C. and Thomson-salo, F. (1997) 'Infant-led innovations in a mother-baby therapy group.' *Journal of Child Psychotherapy* 23, 2, 219–244.

Winnicott, D. (1988) *Babies and Their Mothers*. London: Free Association Books.

CHAPTER 9

Moving Bodies

Dance Movement Psychotherapy Groups for Mothers and Babies
in Inpatient and Outpatient Perinatal Mental Health Services

Marina Rova and Sarah Haddow

In this chapter we discuss how mothers with mental health problems
have used Dance Movement Psychotherapy (DMP) in mother baby
groups to explore their feelings and diverse stories of isolation, guilt
and love. Supporting mothers' interaction with their babies, whilst
attending to subtle nuances of non-verbal communication, creates
opportunities for spontaneous joint movement and promotes bonding
and attachment. The groups we discuss took place in an inpatient
psychiatric mother and baby unit, and in a community setting.

A MOTHER AND BABY INPATIENT UNIT

The stories I (Marina Rova) present are situated within a specialist
National Health Service (NHS) perinatal mental health service in
East London. I am employed under the Arts Therapies department,
offering individual and group inpatient and outpatient DMP. The
Mother and Baby Unit is one of the acute mental health wards in

the psychiatric hospital. An award-winning service, the Mother and Baby Unit comprises 12 inpatient beds and is serviced by a highly skilled multi-disciplinary team including nursing and medical staff, occupational therapy, arts therapies, clinical psychology, parent-infant psychotherapy, social work, midwifery, life skills recovery work and pharmacy. The service accommodates mothers experiencing moderate to severe mental health difficulties during their pregnancy or within the first year after childbirth. This family-centred service aims to support women who require psychiatric treatment to remain with their baby and thus establish their bond. The DMP group was introduced by me in 2010.

MOVEMENT AS COMMUNICATION

The wheels of my trolley rattled as I pushed it down the long hospital corridor. The tambourine cymbals, from within the instrument bag, chimed to the rhythm of my footsteps. At the end of the corridor one hand pressed the security button, the other pushed the trolley forward, followed by a leg used as a doorstop before finally pulling the trolley through. A member of staff happened to come through the other side and joined my 'door dance', mirroring my movements on the opposite side of the trolley, while we smiled. Exchanges like this remind me that movement is at the heart of all communication.

As babies we communicate our needs non-verbally through movement and sound (Amighi, Loman and Sossin 1998), and through movement we become aware of our experiences in the world (Vermes 2011). This innate capacity to experience and communicate through our moving body continues to evolve and transform over our life span.

Attending (and responding) to moving bodies in relationship is a core clinical intervention within the DMP approach. In the context of the Mother and Baby group the 'moving bodies' in question include clinicians, patients and their babies. For example, one can easily make a distinction between the way clinicians and mothers carry themselves across the space. The clinicians often move with a fast-paced rhythm, as they busily attend to their multiple tasks. It may be suggested that clinicians' non-verbal communication indicates a 'being on the move' and 'doing' attitude. On the other hand, patients often move at a slower (more sustained) tempo as their attention is on recovering and, figuratively speaking, finding their feet again.

Babies use their bodies as their primary communication tool. Babies' pre-verbal presence in the space demands that both the clinicians and the mothers attend to their subtle nuances of expression and communication in order to fulfil their basic needs of nourishment, safety, comfort and love (Gerhardt 2014). Below, I offer a snapshot of the inpatient DMP group in action.

BEFORE THE DMP SESSION

DMP sessions were available as an open inpatient therapeutic group to all mothers and babies on the ward. In preparation for the session, I went around the ward inviting mothers to the group, which was due to start in 30 minutes, and took the 'temperature' of the ward. This informal information gathering, based on noticing sounds, expressions and movement qualities of adults and babies, was complimented by the formal medical input at the nurses' handover with updates on patients' recovery and risks.

In the group space, I rearranged the furniture to allow for an open, unobstructed area in the middle of the room. I covered the floor with soft mats, blankets and cushions to create a safe, padded area that encouraged movement at all levels. Moses baskets and baby bouncers were available for occasional use by the babies. Movement props, art materials, musical instruments and a selection of recorded music were arranged on a table for optional use during the session.

OPENING CIRCLE

The group session began with an introductory *check-in* where mothers shared updates of their own and baby's progress. Babies were welcomed into the group with a hello song. A guided warm-up followed involving dyadic and group movement explorations. The warm-up was used as a preparatory stage within the therapeutic process. During this phase of the work mothers were encouraged to become aware of their and their baby's moving bodies, their breath and their rhythms. They were also guided through mobilization of different body parts, and engaging in relational interactions in the group through shared movement activity, such as passing objects around the circle, exploring partner work and **mirroring** movements.

DEVELOPING A MOVEMENT THEME IN THE GROUP

A deepening of the group process involved the development of themes as they emerged through participants' movement initiatives in the *here and now*. Elaine, a 40-year-old mother with a high-flying career in corporate management, found it difficult to contribute to the shared group movements. She told the group she did not know how to play.

Opening up Elaine's theme to the group, mothers explored play in relation to each other and through bonding interactions with their babies. For example, mothers explored playful movement improvisation using a scarf (e.g. peek-a-boo, waving the scarf to create a breeze, cuddling with baby under the scarf). These interactions encouraged mothers to experience their own spontaneity and playfulness, whilst creating a shared movement experience with their baby. Such enactive approaches are especially helpful for depressed mothers who may otherwise have reduced interactions with their babies.

When we revisited Elaine's concern of not knowing how to play, she reflected that her lack of spontaneity extended to other areas of her life. Thus the mother made a connection with a personal theme (lack of spontaneity in her life) and related this to her interpersonal experience with baby (not knowing how to play). The **creative process** had helped the mother to make sense and link her movement experience to how she thought about herself, and so to integrate thoughts and feelings.

FEELING SAFE AND BEING SEEN

A core aim of the inpatient DMP group was to offer a sense of safety to mothers, a feeling of being held, so that they might in turn hold their baby physically, mentally and emotionally' (Loman and Sossin 2009). The DMP group process also encouraged mothers to see (and be seen by) their babies and others. This *seeing* happens within the shared kinaesthetic (the sensory experience of movement) exchange of dyadic and group improvisational dance movement. Movement synchronicity (moving together) and mirroring (echoing each other's movements) are two examples where this *seeing* becomes possible. The therapist resonates with the client's movement and by amplification (i.e. highlighting the quality, rhythm and affective content), she supports the individual to become aware of their embodied expression and hence look at their experience, whilst being seen by another (the therapist and other group members).

AMELIA AND JACK'S DANCE

Amelia and Jack were always first to arrive in the group. Amelia, a young mother with her first child, had only recently come to this country, when the collapse of her relationship with Jack's father triggered her suicide attempt. Amelia did not say a lot in the sessions; she was self-conscious about her limited English. The non-verbal interactions explored in the group seemed to support Amelia to engage in the work in a more immediate and non-threatening way, one that was less demanding than having to talk.

On his part, Jack was mostly alert and responsive; a content baby boy. Jack's excited vocalizations and giggles were often met with his mother's warm smile and gentle caresses, as she reciprocated his communication. The pair shared precious moments of connection during the sessions, predominately through gaze and touch; however, I was aware that Amelia's voice was missing from these exchanges.

THE STRETCH CLOTH: CREATING A COMMON SPACE

The group was exploring the 'giant stretch cloth'. Each mother in turn placed her baby in the cloth and, supported by me, rocked the baby whilst singing a song. Amelia was keen to have a go with Jack. Physical and emotional holding is an important psychological need, crucial for a baby's development (Loman and Sossin 2009; Gerhardt 2014). In this playful exploration I was supporting (and 'holding') Amelia so that she could in turn 'hold' Jack. An additional function of the use of the cloth in this way was that it promoted trust and safety. Amelia and I started to rock Jack in the cloth; however, Amelia's voice was still missing, as she stayed silent.

HELPING AMELIA FIND HER VOICE

Mirroring Amelia's rhythm, I punctuated the silence and followed the movement with a rhythmic 'whoooshhhh...whoooshhh' as Jack swayed from side to side. Amelia looked at me and smiled. Then she joined in, 'whoooshhhh...whoooshhh'. Gradually other mothers joined in, echoing the same sound. The energy in the room shifted. The sound grew across the space and in turn the movement was amplified by the sound. Mothers and babies swayed, rocked, vocalized and laughed. I invited mothers to try out new sounds, and we became more playful, relaxed and experimental.

Amelia now took an initiative and changed the sound. At the same time she started bouncing Jack in the cloth gently, now introducing a new movement quality and relational possibility into their exchange. In response, Jack kicked his legs in the cloth with excitement. Mother and baby giggled together and moved in synchrony, as new sounds echoed from different corners of the room. For the first time Amelia's voice had been heard in the group.

REFLECTION

During the closing circle the mothers shared their difficulty of putting feelings, such as 'isolation', 'anxiety' and 'pain', into words; Amelia nodded in agreement. The shared movement had strengthened her sense of belonging in this group. As the session came to an end I invited all to share one last dance with their baby to a song nominated by the group. The mothers chose 'Songbird'. I was moved to hear Amelia join in the chorus as she rocked baby Jack in her arms. The creative movement process had helped this mother to become more playful and freed her to express her love to her son more fully.

HOSPITAL SETTING: ENCOURAGING A SHARED DANCE BETWEEN MOTHER AND BABY

RELATIONSHIP WITH THE SPACE AND THE PROFESSIONALS IN THE UNIT

In the account that follows Sarah Haddow explores her adapted DMP practice for mothers and babies transitioning from inpatient work towards the changing possibilities within community mental health settings.

I began my career as a DMP in the specialist mother and baby inpatient unit, Rock a Bye Baby (South West England), originally founded by Lucy Livingstone. I have now transferred my knowledge and skills to my current work being part of an interdisciplinary community team, working with Make a Move Charity founded by Michelle Rochester, health visitors and the Local Authority's Active Lifestyle Team. Our focus is on collaboratively supporting mothers, babies and families affected by postnatal depression.

My first step was to transform the emotional climate in the therapy space with blankets for the floor, pillows, colourful fabric, disco lights, bubbles and small musical instruments. I chose not to have chairs in the room – to encourage mothers and babies to be close to each other at ground level. I had learned from Lucy Livingstone that all relationships a woman develops, including direct and indirect contacts, are an integral part of the mother and baby's journey, from receptionist, to the health care assistants, psychiatrists, mental health nurses and the unit manager. My relationships with staff members became stronger as months went by. Often, when I arrived the therapy space had already been set up by staff and patients, which allowed us to co-construct the beginnings of the session and to diffuse feelings of nervousness and anxiety. The attention at this point was solely on supporting mothers to come into the communal space and join in the therapy session.

Ana, a first-time mother of a one-year-old, suffered from postnatal depression:

> My first experience of motherhood wasn't quite the dream I'd hoped for. I was riddled with anxiety and barely able to give my baby a feed. I felt I failed as a mother, and did not understand what was happening to me and why.

Ana was attracted to the DMP session by the music and attended the group with her baby for five weeks.

On many occasions encouraging mothers into the group space was difficult. One mother, Becky, wanted to attend; however, she seemed flat, her face was without expression, her eyes were glazed over, and her self-awareness and attunement with her baby was limited. I sat with her initially, spending time talking with her and her baby and trying to establish a personal contact between us. Each week I repeated this, until one week she came into the therapy space. Trust is an essential element in building relationships, and to encourage mothers to engage (Loman and Sossin 2009).

ALLOWING THE EXPERIENCE OF FEELINGS

Initially I asked Ana to hold her baby gently, to look at her and to respond to what her baby was initiating. When her baby stretched, Ana would mirror her; if her baby made a noise, Ana would make the same noise, whilst maintaining eye contact. These moments of close connection allowed her to feel safe enough and to experience *a rush of love.* She said: 'When you asked us to move with the music and watch our babies' expression, it was liberating and for the very first time I could feel love for my baby.'

One week I asked Ana if there was a song she or her baby loved. I then played it for her and suggested that she move with her baby, finding a rocking rhythm that suited them both. This is Ana's recollection: 'To move gently with my baby, to feel safe, and most importantly just to feel.'

MOVING ON UP: FAMILIES

I moved on to work within a community-based project. It offered perinatal mental health services for mothers with their babies. Together with a multi-disciplinary team, we created a hub of communication and a holding space for mothers with mild to moderate depression, to feel better about themselves and, in turn, to relate better with their babies. Within two years the service, offering ten week-long programmes, had been attended by over 150 mothers. Mothers were supported by our administrator, from the point of referral, and by health visitors through to when they met us for the first time. Cross-collaboration with other professionals is at the heart of the project's success, as our shared learning helps us to better support mothers to recover, grow their sense of self-worth and strengthen their family relationships:

> I watched the transformation of women who allow themselves to express their emotions and whose hope grew with their ability to reach out to each other in the group. I learned to see other professionals' perspectives on what was happening in the **therapeutic space**. (Robyn Pound, Health Visitor)

THE TECHNIQUE OF THE BODY SCAN AND ITS IMPACT

Depending on the mothers' presentation, a guided body scan (Segal, Williams and Teasdale 2012) was facilitated as part of the therapeutic process. This exercise invited mothers to *check in* with each part of their body and to become aware of their feelings, whilst observing the rhythm of their breath. I also encouraged mothers to elongate their breath, which in turn enabled them to feel calmer and less agitated: 'The combination of music and movement, and quiet mindfulness, helped me to reconnect my body and mind' (Lauren).

During discussions following the movement explorations mothers discovered commonalities between each other and developed a feeling of mutual understanding of each other's experiences (Fischman 2009). Relationships developed between mothers over time. Through movement, we explored why mothers felt exhausted and the need for hope was acknowledged. Mothers also expressed a sense of loss for the woman they had been before they had a child.

The movement activities allowed many subtle moments of connection between mother and baby to be recognized and enjoyed together. On one memorable occasion the group came together finding a bouncing quality in their bodies, slowly building a rhythm together, each mother holding her baby. In a circle we all looked across the group. We sang tunes and rhymes, and changed the bounce to a swing and so created a feeling of togetherness through the shared movement and the eye contact. In these moments I responded to what I saw the babies were doing: 'Look, did you see Isla smile?' Mother Sophie, who had been preoccupied until then, raised her head and smiled in return. At that moment she noticed the detail of her baby's expression.

CREATING A SAFE SPACE TO BE TOGETHER

On another occasion, I invited all mothers to lie down with their babies, somewhere comfortable and safe. With Robyn, the health visitor, we floated a large piece of chiffon above them, up and down like a gentle wave. I asked mothers to tune in with their babies and to think what they would like to say and what they thought baby would reply. Marie and Lauren were exhausted and anxious and unable even to name how they were feeling. Marie began to cry when I asked, 'What did you

say to your baby?' She replied, 'I said, sorry.' When asked what baby said back, she responded, 'I love you.'

REFLECTION

The movement experience had allowed Marie to become aware and accepting of herself, and so to connect equally to her feelings of guilt and of love towards her baby. She was able to express these feelings, rather than deny or repress them, because she had an experience of a nurturing environment, which encouraged her to relax, explore and just be with her baby.

Many mothers continued their relationships outside of 'Moving on Up: families' sessions. The group had become a supportive community: 'Getting to know these amazingly strong and honest mummies has undoubtedly helped my recovery and offered me reassurance' (Marie).

CONCLUSION

In this chapter, we have described Dance Movement Psychotherapy work with mothers experiencing mental health problems and who live with their babies in in-patient units or in the community. We are helping them to connect with their babies through movement, body and breath awareness, and then to make sense of their movement experience with words. The felt experience of moving together in synchrony contributes to the mothers and babies developing a movement dialogue, opening the way to develop happier and healthier relationships.

The groups help mothers to build a sense of worth; the commitment to others in the group grows in tandem with improving their relations with their babies. The communal experience of moving together and sharing their feelings also supports women who may feel isolated or fragmented to reconnect with others in the social world around them.

REFERENCES

Amighi, J.K., Loman, S. and Sossin, K.M. (1998) *The Meaning of Movement: Developmental and Clinical Perspectives of the Kestenberg Movement Profile.* New York: Brunner-Routledge.

Fischman, D. (2009) 'Therapeutic Relationships and Kinesthetic Empathy.' In S. Chaiklin and H. Wengrower (eds) *The Art and Science of Dance/Movement Therapy: Life Is Dance.* London: Routledge.

Gerhardt, S. (2014) *Why Love Matters: How Affection Shapes a Baby's Brain.* 2nd edn. London: Routledge.

Loman, S. and Sossin, K.M. (2009) 'Applying the Kestenberg Movement Profile in Dance/Movement Therapy.' In S. Chaiklin and H. Wengrower (eds) *The Art and Science of Dance/Movement Therapy: Life Is Dance.* London: Routledge.

Segal, Z.V., Williams, J.M.G. and Teasdale, J.D. (2012) *Mindfulness-Based Cognitive Therapy for Depression: A New Approach to Preventing Relapse.* 2nd edn. New York: The Guilford Press.

Vermes, K. (2011) Review of *The Corporeal Turn: An Interdisciplinary Reader*, by Maxine Sheets-Johnstone. *Body, Movement and Dance in Psychotherapy* 6, 3, 259–263.

CHAPTER 10

Who Helps Whom?

A Group Analytic Approach to Working with Mothers and
Babies in an NHS Perinatal Mental Health Service

Sheila Ritchie

*As soon as they see the words 'mental health' on my file everything changes. They
start to talk to my husband as if I can't make decisions for myself. Some don't even
look me in the eye. It's as if they are frightened of catching some horrible disease.*

The North East London Foundation Trust (NELFT) Perinatal Parent
Infant Mental Health Service is an integrated tier 3 specialist multi-
disciplinary NHS service. I have run the 'Getting to Know You Group'
in the team since 2010 and this chapter is based on the co-constructed
experience of working with mothers and babies in the group over
that period.

THE CONTEXT FOR THE GROUP

Run at a children's centre on a weekly slow open basis (not time
limited), the group's simple aim is to help women feel less isolated
and share experiences of becoming a mother. Women join then

leave when things have improved, allowing new members to join at different stages. Potential group members find it helpful to hear that the group is only open to women referred to our service. They often assume that all the other mothers in the *regular* groups seem to be doing fine compared with them.

Most mothers referred, and often their partner, have a diagnosis of a serious mental illness. For others the pregnancy or birth has triggered a puerperal psychosis or psychotic depression or a complex response to a traumatic birth. Most women in the group have concurrent psychiatric help from the service.

Multi-disciplinary discussions take place within the team. Working alongside social care and attending child protection meetings are a key part of the therapist's role, which helps hold the tension in assessing both parenting capacity and risk.

Babies, including antenatally, remain central in all discussions and are our patients in their own right with separate electronic case records from birth.

THE GETTING TO KNOW YOU GROUP

- The group meets weekly for 90 minutes, with me as the sole conductor.

- I meet with mother and baby (and partner, if possible) for at least one session prior to joining the group.

- Mothers can join during pregnancy, usually in the third trimester or postnatally, and can stay until babies are about two years old.

- With no formal structured activity, all group members influence what gets talked about in the group. We all stay together for the entirety of the session.

- Spontaneous play in the session allows babies to express what cannot yet be put into words. Using a toy may be a baby's way of commenting about what is happening.

- Rules are different from adult therapy groups: women may have contact outside the group.

- As the only person who attends every session, I provide the consistency, keep the group themes alive and ensure absent members are kept in mind.

- Touching the babies is a common feature of the group as babies use not only their mother's body but also those of other members and the therapist. Adults do not touch each other.

Broadly speaking, the group is influenced by ideas from **group analysis** and parent infant therapy. Change occurs at different levels, which Jones (2006, p.301) usefully categorizes as: 'Firstly, the level of observable behaviors between baby and parent and what the behaviors mean; secondly, hypotheses about the influence of unconscious processes; and thirdly, the level of conscious narrative construction between therapist, parent/s and baby.'

In adult work past difficulties in relationships are largely reported in the present through the reconstruction of memory. In the Getting to Know You Group we often have the opportunity to witness the difficulties in the mother-baby relationship in real time. The mother's difficulties and attachment style, and the potential for this to become the baby's developing attachment style, become evident as the difficulties unfold in the group.

What a group analyst brings to this kind of group is the training to hold in mind the complexity of the different sets of relationships in the group; to keep in mind the group process and themes over time and to work with unconscious processes, whether by putting these into words or not in the group. At times the work takes place in the group analyst's mind.

THERAPIST FLEXIBILITY – LIKE A 'GOOD ENOUGH' PARENT

Working clinically in this area requires an adaptation of any theoretical model, and usual boundaries in adult work are extended. The intimate nature of the work requires flexibility. In the group I may hold babies at times or help wipe up sick. Around the time of the birth we keep in touch by phone or I do home visits.

The work has a profound quality where we may witness a toddler taking their first steps or uttering first words. Strong real attachments form between babies and myself; these can help therapeutic change to occur quite quickly and the aim is to bring the baby's focus back to their mother.

THE IMPACT OF WORKING WITH RISK

As therapists we hear about disturbing fantasies in the mother's mind and help her make sense of these to avoid the risk of acting on these fantasies. In other settings these can become concretized due to an anxiety about risk. The work in a multi-disciplinary team helps share this risk whilst holding psychiatric/psychotherapeutic tensions.

Working with babies activates intense feelings about how we were responded to ourselves as babies. These processes occur either consciously or unconsciously, and as professionals we are not immune to them. To be put in touch as a professional with our own early baby self provides an opportunity to understand this better. Sometimes this can feel too raw and unwelcome, resulting in an urge to take action rather than think about the emotional experience, in order to tolerate uncertainty in the assessment of risk.

A community mental health nurse described her reaction after a home visit of a mother with a diagnosis of personality disorder who was struggling with her newborn baby: 'I was driving faster than usual and felt really wound up. A driver pushed in front of me suddenly and I wound down the window and swore at him. I never usually behave like that!' Team members in this field commonly report levels of rage that feel out of character, in identification with the dysregulated mother or baby, or feeling powerless, trapped and unable to move, in identification with the dependent baby. Feelings generated in the work are often akin to those a partner, mother, baby or grandmother might have.

WORKING WITH EVERYDAY CONCERNS THERAPEUTICALLY

The group material is often focused on everyday aspects of parenting and experiences at different milestones in the babies' development. It can sound just like any other mother and baby group at times. With a more therapeutically oriented group I respond to these concerns with subtlety, without using therapeutic jargon. The rationale is that the past is likely to repeat itself in the present, the repetition being linked to how the mother herself has been parented and her parents parented before her. This is explained by the metaphors of 'ghosts in the nursery' (Fraiberg, Adelson and Shapiro 1975) and 'angels in the nursery' (Lieberman *et al.* 2005). Increasing self-awareness can minimize the potential harm of repetition and allow babies to be freed from negative attributions. Encouraging mothers to show curiosity about the inner workings of the babies' minds can help improve parental **reflective functioning** (Slade 2005).

Often the process of change occurs when first both therapist and group members tune in to the mother's distress, giving space to recognize a feeling not yet acknowledged. Having the chance to express what is going on for her, the mother can begin to soften, and is then better able to respond to her baby.

FEAR OF DOING DAMAGE – 'I SWORE I NEVER WOULD BUT I'M FRIGHTENED THAT I AM TURNING INTO MY MOTHER!'

DYSREGULATION, CONFUSION AND ISOLATION
AT THE START OF THE GROUP

A mother, Wanda, had presented to the service with a fear of becoming a bad mother. She had experienced inadequate parenting with sexual and physical abuse as a child and had a diagnosis of emotionally unstable personality disorder.

Wanda arrived late with her seven-month-old baby Milly, flustered and frustrated; cuddled her briefly, then placed her in the circle at a distance from her. This was unusual. She looked visibly distressed. It was not clear why she kept her baby Milly at a distance. Was she seeking some relief from her demands or trying to protect her baby from her, allowing her daughter to have contact with another mother, whom she thought would do a better job?

PAST AND PRESENT COLLAPSE IN THE MOMENT

Wanda described how Milly's bottle had been leaking so she had bought a new brand. Her baby had refused to feed from it this morning. She was struggling to wean Milly, even though she had been encouraged to start offering solids. She had felt criticized by health visitors for having a bottle that leaked. She said she felt ashamed as she had tried to be patient and could not understand why Milly would not take the milk like she usually did. Then she had 'lost it' and shouted at her. This had never happened before.

She started to cry. One of the other mothers was engaging baby Milly with a toy as she spoke. Wanda looked at me and said, 'I don't know what to do now.' I was in touch with her desperation and her longing and dependency on me to make it better by 'feeding her' with the right answer.

Aware of the mother's chronic compulsive eating problem, I suggested that something powerful had happened that morning that perhaps was not just about her daughter not taking the milk but maybe something connected with how she herself had been fed in her early life.

REPARATIVE EXPERIENCE? – THE SAME, OR A DIFFERENT RESPONSE?

Wanda then talked for the first time in the group about being forced when younger to eat food she did not like, until she gagged. She also remembered at other times feeling very hungry, as she was not fed regularly. She was horrified that she had become like her mother in shouting at Milly and hated herself for it. She looked at us sheepishly, as if she expected to be judged by the group, just as her family would have done.

THE GROUP DOES THE WORK – SHARING EXPERIENCES WITH PEERS

Instead of judging, one mother talked about how difficult she had found it when her son had refused to drink from anything but one kind of bottle. She had been 'tearing her hair out not knowing what was wrong', and suggested Wanda change the teat of the old bottle rather than changing the bottle itself. She added that babies could be so powerful in rejecting food when something was wrong and how rejecting of the mother it could feel. I added my own thought that eating was the first thing we learned to control in life and refusal to eat was an early way of protesting when things just did not feel right.

Another mother talked about her own eating problems in the past and how she too had been forced to eat food that she did not like. She then went on to make a connection with her anxiety:

> When I was a compulsive eater I didn't know how to gauge when I was hungry or full. I guess that is why I struggle so much now with the feeding. It feels such a responsibility because they could die if they don't get enough!

A few mothers agreed and went on to share how difficult it was for them to give up breastfeeding or the bottle, when they had taken such pleasure in it, as they felt rejected; as if they were not needed any more when their babies started to eat solids more independently.

GETTING INTO THE MINDS OF THE BABIES

Wanda insisted that Milly just was not ready to eat solid foods yet. She had tried during the week but her daughter had just spat the food out. It transpired that she had given her porridge but had not added salt or sugar as they were bad for her. Someone responded gently, 'I don't blame her! It won't taste of anything! I usually mash up banana in mine.'

BABIES HELP EACH OTHER IN THE GROUP

A 15-month-old boy, Joshua, went over to his mother. Sensing that he was hungry, she gave him a small snack. Milly looked towards her with interest. She checked with Wanda if it was okay for Milly to have some. Wanda hesitated but then agreed. Joshua's mother said, 'Shall we give Milly a bit?' Joshua moved towards Milly with his own piece in one hand and gave a bit to her with the other. Milly picked it up, smelled it, got it between her fingers with intense concentration then sucked it. The group was transfixed in silence, giving space and attention to her exploration. I encouraged Wanda to move closer so she could watch what was happening. Milly was clearly enjoying the new sensation, making appreciative noises. Wanda smiled, visibly moved, and was able to reflect on the difference between herself as a child and Milly. Milly was being uninhibited and allowed to explore with her own hands and at her own pace something she, Wanda, had never been allowed to do.

SEPARATING OUT PAST FROM PRESENT

As the session progressed and we moved on to other things Wanda was able to reclaim her baby and they had some moving, playful interactions. At the next session Wanda told us that she had been enjoying experimenting, cooking new foods for Milly, and reported, 'She is learning what she wants in life!'

REFLECTION

Wanda felt misunderstood by the professionals' not recognizing the roots of her difficulty, which left her feeling inadequate and confused about why she was struggling with something apparently so basic. She expected to be judged for her inadequacies not only by the professionals but also by the group, just as in her family.

In the group we are repeatedly forced to witness distressing moments when a mother's response to her baby is less than adequate. This is difficult to bear at times but what is crucial is persevering with trying to understand the difficulty. If we can trust the group process, what unfolds over time is how the mother herself was mothered.

It often comes as a relief to have normalized a tendency to revert to saying the things that our mothers once said to us. We often hear, 'I couldn't help myself! It just came out of my mouth!' Feelings of guilt about inadequacies often get voiced in the group. Where there is a resistance to change over time, interventions to protect the baby from the potential damage do need to be considered. In cases where a mother has good intentions and a willingness to change, she can learn a lot from others in the group.

Rather than castigating themselves, the mothers are encouraged to think about the inevitability of ruptures in parenting and that what is crucial is the way in which ruptures can get repaired. Perhaps in all parenting there is a tension between **repetition compulsion** (Freud and Freud 2001) and an opportunity through parenting to repair earlier experiences.

BABIES AS EQUAL GROUP MEMBERS AND CONTRIBUTORS

This example demonstrates how babies are active and equal participants and their contributions crucial for the functioning of the group. The innocent forgiving gaze or longing of one baby often stirs maternal feelings in another mother unable to feel these feelings for her own baby. This is when a baby can offer something more powerful than any therapist.

Babies often initiate encounters, which are meaningful, as Milly and Joshua did in the example above. This helps mothers consider that they too may have been uninhibited at this age and that something has happened to make them less likely to trust and want to make social connections.

The long slow open nature of the group means that more experienced members, mothers and older babies alike, help the newer members develop, remembering what it was like when they were struggling, giving hope that if they stick at coming to the group, however difficult they find it, that it is possible that things can improve.

'CLAIMING THE BABY'

Many mothers find it hard to believe that they are the most important person in their baby's life. Through the group they can begin to see that whilst their baby is capable of seeking out contact with a range of people, ultimately they will have a preference for mother (James 2016).

One mother, who was planning to give her baby up for adoption, looked on as I engaged her baby and he smiled and babbled at me as I talked with him. The mother was convinced that he preferred me, just as she felt that her baby preferred her own mother. I told the mother that he was smiling at me because I was talking with him, and I spoke with the baby about how he was trying so hard to let his mother know how important she was to him but she was struggling to believe this. I encouraged the mother to practise chatting to him about everyday things and the following session she reported really enjoying the connection. Their relationship began to improve and she went on to keep him.

Change often occurs non-verbally through imitation and **mirroring**. One mother's stroke of her baby's head finds its way travelling round the group, quite unconsciously. Often a deadness or isolation at the start of a session changes to something more alive and social. Both babies' and mothers' faces light up as in unspoken recognition, and multiple connections can get made. We create the conditions for Foulkes's (1984) 'hall of mirrors' to happen, where each group member finds a range of mirrors in other group members to help discover who they are through both similarities and differences.

THINKING ABOUT DISTURBED FEELINGS

Bringing a range of disturbance into the group can create an anxiety in the therapist about what we might be exposing mothers and babies to. Encouraging difficulties to be talked about freely can prove fruitful to the group's functioning. When one mother can take a risk, such as Wanda telling the group that she shouted at Milly and was on the verge of force-feeding her, others will usually follow, finding an opportunity to reveal their own untold fears.

Sharing the experience of being a mother can be a great leveller so that women from all walks of life from asylum seekers to high-powered professionals can help each other. Group dynamics of competition and envy can usually be put aside, in order to privilege the shared need for understanding and acceptance and the shame at not feeling good enough.

THE POTENTIAL FOR CHANGE IN THE GROUP

Change is not always easy and not every mother can be helped to do an adequate job as a parent. The women in the example I have used were motivated to change, did not want to repeat their own childhood experience and had the potential to tune in to their babies' needs, with the help of the group. Due to the plasticity of babies' brains, problems in attachment have the potential to be resolved quite quickly. Helping each other, the mothers can grow in confidence and feel a sense that they matter. They often gain an awareness of their own authority as they develop more confidence in being a mother. They can start to translate this to groups outside and find it easier to function at work, in the family and in social situations.

Babies get to see others their own size, build confidence, and discover that they too have something to offer and some agency to have an impact on others. As younger babies join, older babies have to learn to be gentle, and to share and cooperate. They learn to use a group situation with peers, a life skill that can potentially compensate for difficult experiences at home or in relationships throughout their lives.

I am grateful to all the mothers and babies I have worked with who have taught me so much, not only about the work, but also about myself.

REFERENCES

Foulkes, S.H. (1984) *Therapeutic Group Analysis*. London: Maresfield Reprints.

Fraiberg, S., Adelson, E. and Shapiro, V. (1975) 'Ghosts in the nursery.' *Journal of the American Academy of Child Psychiatry 14*, 3, 387–421.

Freud, S. and Freud, A. (2001) *The Standard Edition of the Complete Psychological Works of Sigmund Freud. Vol 20: 'An autobiographical study', 'inhibitions', 'symptoms and anxiety', 'lay analysis' and Other Works*. Ed. James Strachey. London: Vintage Classics.

James, J. (2016) 'Parent-Infant Psychotherapy in Groups.' In T. Baradon with M. Biseo, C. Broughton, J. James and A. Joyce *The Practice of Psychoanalytic Parent-Infant Psychotherapy: Claiming the Baby*. 2nd edn. London: Routledge.

Jones, A. (2006) 'Levels of change in parent-infant psychotherapy.' *Journal of Child Psychotherapy 32*, 3, 295–311.

Lieberman, A.F., Padrón, E., Van Horn, P. and Harris, W.W. (2005) 'Angels in the nursery: the intergenerational transmission of benevolent parental influences.' *Infant Mental Health Journal 26*, 6, 504–520.

Slade, A. (2005) 'Parental reflective functioning: an introduction.' *Attachment & Human Development 7*, 3, 269–281.

CHAPTER 11

When the Bough Breaks

The Lighthouse Programme

Gerry Byrne and Gabrielle Lees

The Lighthouse© MBT-Parenting Programme is a **mentalization-based group treatment (MBT)** for parents where there are significant safeguarding concerns. Their children may be at high risk of abuse or re-abuse, on child protection plans, involved with family courts or already placed in the care of the Local Authority. Although the groups usually take place without any children present, this chapter will consider how the presence of a baby, in utero and/or in person can impact on the group dynamics, the other parents and the facilitators.

The Lighthouse model has been developed in collaboration with the Anna Freud Centre, and adapted to incorporate therapeutic methods and skills from **mentalization-based treatment**, developed by Anthony Bateman and Peter Fonagy (Bateman and Fonagy 2008).

CONTEXT

The Lighthouse Programme is delivered by the National Health Service (NHS) in a specialist child and adolescent mental health service (CAMHS). The aim of the service is to offer intervention to parents and their children to break the cycle of repeated abuse and/or neglect and trans-generational cycles of attachment difficulties and lifelong psychological difficulties. It includes psycho-education, group therapy and individual treatment. The Lighthouse© MBT-Parenting Programme has been developed specifically to promote mentalizing (the ability to imagine, to perceive and to interpret other people's behaviour in terms of deliberate mental states, such as feelings and intentions [Stolk *et al.* 2007]) in parents whose children have been identified as in danger of, or have already experienced, emotional and physical maltreatment, abuse and neglect. The programme aims to improve parental functioning and strengthen the parent-child relationship. This is achieved by educating parents to mentalize, think about feelings and intentions, their own and their child's, to help them understand the child's mind, enhance their sensitivity and empathy, and improve attunement to their baby. This offers greater opportunity for developing a more 'secure' attachment and reducing the likelihood of abuse in the future. In our experience, it is failures in a parent's mentalizing capacity, usually in moments of high stress, such as hearing a baby cry inconsolably, that can result in serious physical or psychological harm to the baby.

The parents we work with have almost always been traumatized by their experiences in childhood, and their histories of neglect, physical, sexual and/or emotional abuse often result in serious personality problems, mental health difficulties or substance abuse. A number of parents attending the programme have lost children to care recently, some have their children currently in foster care and others may lose care of their baby or children during the treatment period. Many groups contain at least one pregnant mother and sometimes the baby, once born, attends with the mother for the remaining weeks.

In her paper 'Ghosts in the nursery', Selma Fraiberg (Fraiberg, Adelson and Shapiro 1975) describes a young mother who is apparently deaf to her baby's cries. She concludes that the mother's cries went unheard when she was a baby herself. Parents we work with show numerous blind spots to their children's communications and so struggle to hold their children in mind and respond to them sensitively and appropriately.

GROUP STRUCTURE

The Lighthouse group component runs for a minimum of 20 weeks and is facilitated by two or three experienced therapists with between 8 and 14 parents – about half of whom will be couples. The programme is popular with families and other professionals and since 2015 has been manualized (researched and giving step-by-step instructions for implementation).

The group is held weekly for two hours, and the first 12–15 weeks include psycho-educational material aimed at promoting mentalizing of the child in the parent's mind. Key concepts from attachment and psychoanalytic theory are explained and it is made clear to all that the main aim of treatment is to enable parents to better mentalize, and to recognize when they are not-mentalizing. Methods include group discussions, role plays, using images and metaphors, videos and group exercises. The participants are given a Lighthouse Journal, which summarizes the content of the programme and can be used at home or in sessions to record personal reflections.

BABIES AND THE LIGHTHOUSE GROUP

We do not have babies in the group as a matter of course. This is because we cannot usually afford crèches. When we have, these have been ideal opportunities to practise separations and reunions safely and thoughtfully. The Lighthouse Programme contains significant amounts of educational content, which requires full concentration, is emotive and can be disturbing for parents as they struggle to understand and name their feelings.

Despite our 'rule' of no babies, we find that in most groups at least one baby attends at some point, either in utero or after they have just been born (sometimes they can be under a week old). As the majority of our parents have at least one child under the age of two, we encourage parents to think and talk about them throughout the programme and they therefore feature significantly even in their absence. We also talk about the babies lost for good in the care system.

At other times when babies are brought in by their parents, we attempt to understand this in terms of group dynamics and the parent's individual therapeutic processes.

EMOTIONAL MIS-ATTUNEMENT IN SIGHT OF THE GROUP

In this example, a new baby was born during the group programme. The parents had another child, an 18-month-old son, Harry who had been placed in foster care due to suspicions of fabricated or induced illness (FII) by Chloe, which was denied by both parents. Harry had been returned to his parents with a tight written agreement that his father, Ash, would take on a greater role in parenting.

Ash was verbose and his manner was at times somewhat intimidating. In contrast, Chloe was very quiet. About half-way through, when the Lighthouse Programme had developed a cohesive and friendly culture, their new baby arrived. The couple arrived proudly with baby Joe who started to cry softly at first, then more loudly, Chloe attempted to settle Joe but could not, and became increasingly stressed and tearful. After what seemed a long time and to everyone's relief, Ash suggested that he would take Joe for a walk to help him get off to sleep.

REFLECTION

Ash was able to tolerate far more distress in his baby than Chloe (and more, too, than the group and facilitators). In team supervision we reflected on how hard it had been for Chloe to come into the room very excited to be showing off her new baby only to find that in front of an 'audience' she was unable to soothe him. Her discomfort at feeling watched and judged led her to become increasingly tense, which we felt baby Joe picked up on, which increased his sense of panic. Ash was slower than expected to respond, but had managed to take control and soothe Joe relatively quickly. We wondered about the dynamics in the couple, and what the experience may have been like for baby Joe. In our team supervision, we reflected on what part this process contributed to the exaggeration of Harry's symptoms. Chloe, left to parent alone, became overwhelmed but was unable to communicate this to Ash. He in turn was too slow to notice her cues and did not pick up on the sense of urgency, neither from his son's cries, nor from his wife's rising level of distress.

We were able to use reflection to better understand why Harry had come to be harmed. We then engaged further directly with Chloe to help her talk about her anxieties, namely, that there was something 'wrong' with Harry when he was a baby.

BABY INTERACTING WITH OTHER GROUP MEMBERS

Facilitators noted that there was very little interaction between baby Joe and his parents. He did not make eye contact with either parent and nor did they speak with him although he was awake for most of the session. When he was fed a bottle, Joe avoided his mother's gaze throughout and this did not seem to concern her. They were, however, keen for the group to admire Joe and we noticed that he appeared to be looking elsewhere for responsive faces. This resulted in other group members and facilitators instinctively modelling attending to and delighting in Joe. Due to the levels of concern raised in these observations, the facilitators introduced Video Interaction Guidance

(VIG) for Chloe and Joe alongside the group programme. Over the next few weeks these interventions resulted in increased involvement and interest from Ash and Chloe. Baby Joe spent less time averting his gaze and we observed moments of clear attunement and reciprocity.

COMPETITION AND BABY AS SHIELD AGAINST THINKING

In one group, we had two sets of parents where this was played out. Carly and Tom had a nine-month-old daughter, Rosie. Carly had three other children who had been removed to care and there were serious concerns about the parenting of Rosie. The couple lived rather chaotic lives and Carly came from a renowned family network where she had been abused, yet with whom she seemed to remain enmeshed. There were ongoing serious problems including violence, rejection and child neglect.

The previous week, parents had seen video clips, which aroused strong feelings; some parents struggled to control themselves and paced the room or shouted angrily.

This week, Carly brought baby Rosie in, placed her on the floor in front of them and fed her chocolate biscuits and crisps. The couple spent most of the session passing Rosie things, taking photos and videos of her and talking loudly to her. This was difficult for the facilitators, who were concerned about the need to get through the material. They also worried about what Rosie might be exposed to, if like in the previous week parents became visibly upset.

Later when we reflected, we wondered if Carly and Tom had brought Rosie to avoid getting upset. When asked questions, they both made statements such as: 'Sorry, I missed that,' and, 'I didn't hear a word of that because Rosie was pulling my trousers.' A couple of times Rosie shuffled towards another group member, who would lean down and talk to her and she would respond with big open-mouthed smiles. Carly and Tom were delighted with this and we saw that they felt pleased and proud to have their daughter be such a magnet of interest.

They were able to experience a rare moment of being at the centre of positive attention and offering something special to the other group members.

Louise then said that she wished that the group could see her son too and started to show pictures of him on her phone. Facilitators spent time with the group thinking how it felt to want to share their pride with the others. The following week, Rosie was not brought in, but Louise came with her son, clearly dressed in his smartest clothes, saying that she had been let down by her childcare arrangements. We understood this as Louise's wish for her and her son similarly to experience the admiration of the group.

REFLECTION

Both of these parents struggled with regulating their emotions; their relationship with each other and others regularly involved high drama and their lifestyle was chaotic. The previous session had involved a video of a crying baby who was not picked up by his father. We wondered what this may have evoked in Carly and Tom.

In both cases the parents used their babies to regulate their emotions as well as to have their own needs met. In addition, in common with many parents, they craved admiration and approval as parents. Perhaps for Carly and Tom the crying baby without help and soothing connected with their own experiences of neglect and helplessness and they craved the admiration and approval of the group, which they never had received as children.

NOTICING EXTREME BEHAVIOUR AND OFFERING ADDITIONAL INTERVENTIONS

Sometimes our observations of the interaction between parent and child resulted in different outcomes. Louise brought her 13-month-old son, Kye, on more than one occasion. We were struck with how serious and still the baby was. He tended to be left in his buggy for two hours and made few attempts to ask to get out; unusual for a toddler.

Louise showed little interest in him. She faced him away from her and interacted very little; he did not respond to interaction attempts from other parents to make him smile and made few demands. Over time, people stopped trying to engage Kye. This alarmed the facilitators, but Louise, in individual sessions, said that she had no concerns about her son, and would laugh dismissively that he was 'like an old man'. This behaviour, her withdrawal from the programme and her lack of insight resulted in our escalating concerns regarding risk to her baby.

PAIN EVOKED BY SEEING OTHER PARENTS' BABIES

Lucy and Sam were a young couple. They had a year-old baby and when they joined the group Lucy was pregnant with her second. When their firstborn, Max, was three months old, he had been injured on more than one occasion while in his father's care. Sam admitted causing the injuries and was required to move out of the family home while attending the Lighthouse Programme and with further assessment of the risk he posed to his children. Both parents had difficult backgrounds and Sam had himself been physically and emotionally abused as a child and scapegoated within his family.

The couple engaged fully with all interventions and they cherished the 'parental attention' our service provided them with. They became particularly invested in the group and often talked about it being the 'highlight of their week'. Both grew in confidence as parents as the weeks passed.

They shared their excitement about the pregnancy and brought their baby daughter to a group session just three days after the birth. There was much admiration from the other parents and new baby Penny quickly seemed to become a 'group baby', loved by all; however, another single mother in the group, Hannah, felt very differently. A few months previously, she had had a newborn baby removed at birth. At the time, Hannah had been in a violent relationship and drinking heavily.

In her individual work, Hannah had significantly increased her understanding of the role her lifestyle played in her loss of her baby, and discussed how she struggled to interact with or enjoy baby Penny. She said it was painful to see the couple do so well with their baby and share the care between them. She was tearful and said she would have had to be a single parent if she had kept her baby, and that she knew this would have been difficult for her and her baby. As she watched Penny grow over the weeks and saw the pleasure Lucy and Sam derived from her, the more in touch she became with her own loss and the sadder she became.

CONCLUSION

Although they are not officially invited to attend the Lighthouse group, when parents do bring their babies it provides us with live and valuable information and can alter the course of our work in the sessions. Facilitators are mindful of the mixed feelings babies can arouse in group members, especially in those who have lost babies before, and it is important to talk about these feelings both in the group and in individual sessions.

We often discuss the benefits of seeing the parents and their babies together in the group sessions and this leads us to remain open to thinking about our 'rule' of no babies and whether there is a way to incorporate this into the programme – such as through the provision of a crèche facility, which depends on funding. It would be far better to provide parents with opportunities to be in the group both with and at other times without their babies. For some parents, seeing others delight in their baby appears to ignite their own interest and pleasure. It gives them encouragement to interact with their baby more and in turn the baby's responsiveness then contributes to the creation of a joyful cycle of reciprocal interaction.

The Lighthouse© MBT-Parenting Programme's overall aim is to increase parental mentalizing of the child/baby and whether the latter are physically present or absent, the facilitators' task is always to encourage the group to hold the babies in mind.

REFERENCES

Bateman, A. and Fonagy, P. (2008) '8-year follow-up of patients treated for borderline personality disorder: mentalization-based treatment versus treatment as usual.' *American Journal of Psychiatry 165*, 5, 631–638.

Fraiberg, S., Adelson, E. and Shapiro, V. (1975) 'Ghosts in the nursery.' *Journal of the American Academy of Child Psychiatry 14*, 3, 387–421.

Stolk, M.N., Mesman, J., van Zeijl, J., Alink, L.R.A., Bakermans-Kranenburg, M.J., van Ijzendoorn, M.H., Juffer, F. and Koot, H.M. (2007) 'Early parenting intervention: family risk and first-time parenting related to intervention effectiveness.' *Journal of Child and Family Studies 17*, 1, 55–83.

PROGRAMMES

CHAPTER 12

Baby Steps

A Relationship-Based Perinatal Group Programme

Angela Underdown

New parenthood presents a daunting challenge for most men and women and this is even greater when the transition takes place within the context of disadvantage such as poverty, domestic violence and abuse, addiction or a lack of support networks. All parents set out to be the best they can be, and the transition to parenthood offers a window of opportunity when expectant parents are often very receptive to reflecting on how they want to be as parents and what sort of family they want to create. This in turn creates a parallel obligation and responsibility to ensure that perinatal groups offer parents the very best evidence-based support to help them negotiate a healthy transition to parenthood.

This chapter outlines the ethos of a relationship-based perinatal programme that aims to support men and women in their emotional transition to becoming parents.

BACKGROUND

My interest in supporting expectant parents began many years ago when, as a health visitor student, I was asked to participate in leading antenatal classes. I soon discovered that these were mainly didactic advice-giving sessions to large groups of expectant parents, focusing on physical health and doing little to weave together all the threads of emotional change and challenge facing new parents (Underdown 1998a, 1998b). I knew even then that there had to be a better way of approaching this! I became involved both in research about perinatal group programmes and parent-baby interaction and in co-facilitating and developing interactive relationship-based programmes. Change did not happen quickly and research from 2009 (Schrader McMillan, Barlow and Redshaw 2009) indicated that antenatal classes were still medically focused with little emphasis on emotional relationships. In 2011 the National Society for the Prevention of Cruelty to Children (NSPCC) commissioned me to write a preventative perinatal programme for more vulnerable expectant parents.

During the first year, the programme was tested and feedback from parents and facilitators was elicited so that it could be fine-tuned and adapted for different groups. The programme was named Baby Steps. It was offered initially by the NSPCC in nine areas across the UK and in Jersey, and facilitators were trained to deliver it. Currently, the programme is being delivered by the National Health Service (NHS) and Local Authority practitioners, and a facilitator training team is now being developed. In this chapter, the general ethos of the Baby Steps programme is shared and examples from practice are used to illustrate the central themes and approach.

BABY STEPS – THE ETHOS

Baby Steps consists of six two-hour prenatal and three postnatal group meetings. Each nine-week programme is led consistently by two interdisciplinary facilitators drawn from midwifery, social work, health visiting or early years. Once names of potential participants have been received, the facilitators make contact and offer a home visit. This initial contact is the first opportunity to begin to engage with the parents – to 'weave the ethos', the supportive cradle that is the central core of Baby Steps.

Although most facilitators are used to doing perinatal home visits, they are often busy ensuring physical health and wellbeing needs. Baby Steps facilitators like to do a home visit because they recognize the value of taking time to get to know and value their clients, including the unborn babies, as individuals. The relationship-building home visit has helped to engage families who would not usually attend a group meeting at a centre. Parents with previous adverse experience of services combined with chaotic lifestyles may not return telephone calls or keep the appointment time for the home visit. Baby Steps facilitators' persevering with gentle persistence, without showing frustration, is the beginning of consistent commitment to participants and the start of building a trusting relationship.

Facilitators find that parents are more relaxed in their own home and more receptive to exploring the programme because they have 'ownership' of the visit and facilitators are their guests. Baby Steps facilitators use affirming techniques to help relax parents, such as paying attention to the surroundings and commenting positively and with genuine curiosity. Affirming comments must be authentic; for instance, one facilitator remembers how easily she bonded with a young father when she noticed football team colours and said that she too was a fan.

During the home visit, facilitators take time to really listen and attune to the expectant parents' stories, and every effort is made to engage with both partners in a respectful and interested way. Meeting the family in their own surroundings can help with identification and assessment of need. It also enables facilitators to ensure expectant parents receive a warm welcome at the group and that content is adjusted to meet any special needs. One single mother in her early twenties who had experienced depression and anxiety after being in a violent relationship shared how the home visit had made her feel more confident to engage with the group:

> I found the home visit really good. It helped me to feel confident in coming to a group. Facilitators appeared interested in me and listened to my story. They were lovely and definitely made me want to come to the group.

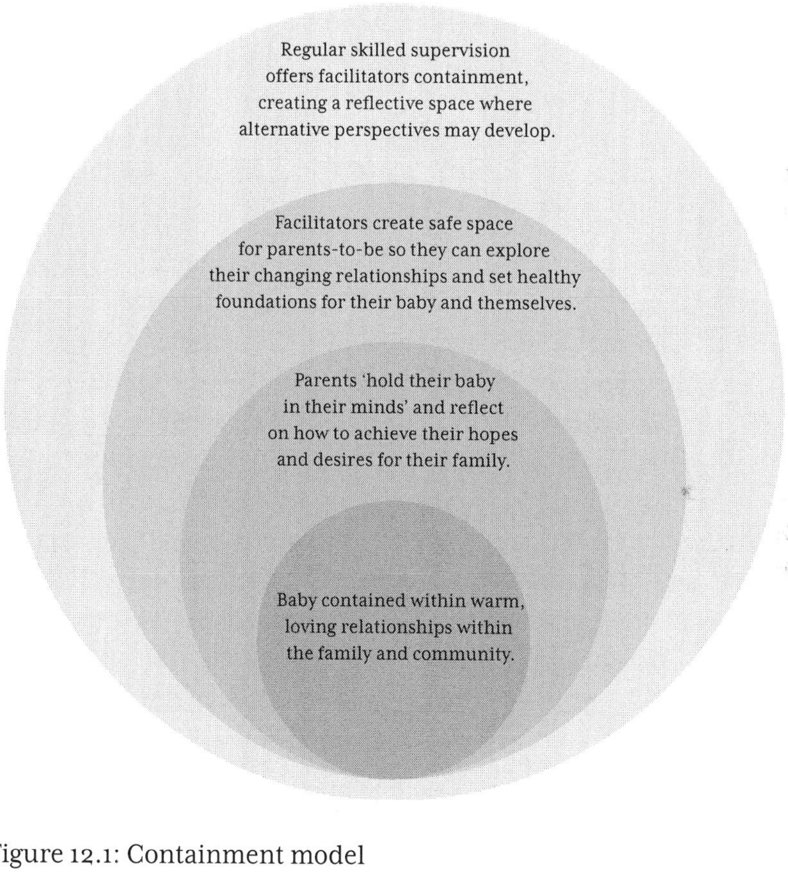

Regular skilled supervision offers facilitators containment, creating a reflective space where alternative perspectives may develop.

Facilitators create safe space for parents-to-be so they can explore their changing relationships and set healthy foundations for their baby and themselves.

Parents 'hold their baby in their minds' and reflect on how to achieve their hopes and desires for their family.

Baby contained within warm, loving relationships within the family and community.

Figure 12.1: Containment model

Parents who have experienced trauma in their lives often find it difficult to build trust. Baby Steps consistently models safe, respectful relationships and offers interactive opportunities to explore and reflect on communication patterns. Each of the group sessions begins with a check-in, giving parents an opportunity to share and update the rest of the group about anything they wish to share. Group boundaries are co-constructed early and parents know each session has a busy, interactive content and that facilitators may need to hear participants but also move on and follow up some issues later.

Thus, the fabric of Baby Steps is implicitly woven with respectful containing relationships while some communication patterns – such as active listening, conflict resolution skills and observing baby cues and sleep/wake states – are explicitly explored. The explicit learnings are activities designed with a specific purpose such as improving listening skills. These activities are directly supported by the ethos of the programme where sensitive, reflective, containing communication patterns are implicitly modelled.

Often, initial contact can be difficult to establish and parents facing additional challenges may have more pressure on their time or may have a mistrust of services. While it is preferable to do this home visit, facilitators are mindful that occasionally parents feel worried about having a professional visit their home and are more relaxed initially to meet on 'neutral' ground such as a coffee shop. This nurturing culture offers parents a safe space where their concerns and difficult feelings can be heard and they will be able to 'hear' and contain their own baby's feelings and individuality. This ethos is encapsulated in the containing model in Figure 12.1.

The next sections highlight examples of how Baby Steps facilitators weave together a) **implicit** and b) **explicit communication** to offer parents a safe space to explore and develop their relationships with their babies and each other.

IMPLICIT COMMUNICATION – USING
PRINCIPLES OF ATTUNEMENT

Within the group setting, facilitators continue to validate parents by being friendly and approachable and observing and remembering personal details that parents have shared. Using the Video Interaction Guidance (VIG) attunement principles (Kennedy, Landor and Todd 2011) as an underlying approach, facilitators model receiving all comments that parents make in a positive and interested way (see also Chapter 6).

This can be challenging when comments may reflect something with which facilitators disagree or even consider harmful. For example, a facilitator recalls a discussion about soothing babies' distress when a father strongly argued that it was important to leave babies to cry otherwise they would become spoilt and not learn how to behave. The group leaders tried to balance upholding babies' needs while not alienating the father and ensuring the rest of the group had the opportunity to reflect. They did this by acknowledging his view and, over several sessions, subtly addressing this from different perspectives such as self-reflection: 'What do we as adults need when we are distressed?'

It was a particular bonus to the two facilitators when the father approached them a few weeks later and said he had been thinking about things he had learnt from the course and he had decided that he would not leave his baby to feel frightened and lonely crying by himself. The facilitators felt validated that they had managed to contain their own anxious feelings and enabled the father to reflect over time. They said they had really learnt to 'trust in the process' of the group and realized that change takes time and comes from the parent's own discovery rather than being 'taught'.

The facilitators commented on the importance of participating in regular, skilled supervision where they shared their concerns and reflected with an experienced mentor who offered **containment** and development of alternative perspectives.

CREATING A SENSE OF BELONGING WITHIN THE GROUP

Part of the implicit group process involves fostering a caring attitude between participants. This group ethos is shown in a variety of ways with facilitators expressing genuine concern if someone expected has not arrived and addressing details to ensure participants' safety and comfort. As participants feel more at ease, there is often a sense of fun and belonging within the group, making it a more relaxed and caring place. The evaluation of Baby Steps (Hogg, Coster and Brookes 2015) found that the majority of parents made new friends in the group and 61 per cent were still in touch six months later:

> I'm always so very excited to come every Tuesday and see the other mums. It's like we're family. I'm so grateful to have met them; we've become so close. If I'm feeling anxious I call them and they calm me down. (Mother – six years in UK)

HOLDING THE UNBORN BABIES IN MIND

The unborn babies are valued in the same way, with facilitators using names (or friendly nicknames) if shared by parents and wondering about individual likes and dislikes. For example, parents are often surprised to know that their unborn baby can hear from around 24 weeks and may enjoy thinking about what sounds their baby may respond to. Unborn babies are never referred to as 'it' by facilitators and, without explicit explanation, expectant parents often copy this respectful way of being.

REDUCING ANXIETY BY SHARING EXPERIENCES

Daniel Stern (1995) first described how expectant mothers may be full of self-doubt, which they are too frightened to share because they fear being judged as 'not good enough'. One expectant mother, who was experiencing anxiety, said she felt guilty because she had not previously been aware that her unborn baby could hear in the womb and that she could make connections. Her group facilitators were aware of the theory and research underpinning the emotional transition to parenthood and they carefully listened and observed so that they could authentically help within an ethos of acceptance and confidence promotion. Within this valuing ethos, the mother was able to reflect on how she held her unborn baby in mind:

> Even though I feel silly I have been speaking to my baby and touching my bump in response to kicks. My partner is working away and I have told him the importance of baby hearing his voice so I have recorded him speaking to the baby when he is on the phone and I play it back to baby.

Feeling able to share what she was actively doing and have this acknowledged by the facilitators helped to lower anxiety and support self-recognition of her unique role.

This expectant mother felt 'safe' to share feeling guilty for not knowing something about her unborn baby and this increased her confidence to connect with her unborn baby (Benoit, Parker and Zeanah 1997). By sharing this in the group, she also realized that most expectant mothers do not automatically know about baby development. Sharing vulnerabilities can help to create a strong, supportive group where individuals feel confident to reflect about their own parenting and how they want to be with their own baby.

MODELLING

A good example of modelling is how a life-like baby massage doll is used to model interaction and care in a number of ways. The doll has a name and is treated respectfully by the group. During the nappy change demonstration, the facilitator talks all the time to the doll as if she were a real baby and answers parents' questions 'through' the doll. This gives a powerful message that caring routines are a special time for uninterrupted communication. When discussions are taking place, the baby doll may be held or cuddled by either facilitators or expectant parents, giving implicit messages about how to handle a real baby. Two facilitators who had just completed the first session of a new programme held and included their doll, Felix, throughout the session and were pleased when they received these comments as parents were leaving:

> I really liked that Felix is part of the group. I found myself watching you with Felix and found it comforting.

> I was wondering as well and learning from you how I should hold a baby.

ENCOURAGING RECIPROCAL INTERACTION

On occasions, facilitators talk directly to the doll to model reciprocity, attunement and regulatory function (Schore and Schore 1999). Many adults are visual learners and modelling responses to the doll's imaginary cues can be amusing but also a powerful and memorable demonstration of reciprocal sensitive interaction.

A mother who had experienced mental ill-health and domestic violence described how this had a powerful effect on how she cared for her baby:

> Watching how the facilitators talked to 'baby' during the bathing exercise made me more aware of talking to my baby when interacting with him. I learnt how to fully engage with my baby when he is awake so that I don't miss anything, keeping myself in the moment. I am especially conscious of doing this during feed times.

Facilitators continually model a group ethos with attuned respectful interactions, and the way they work together to lead the group models a healthy couple relationship.

The next section describes how the Baby Step ethos is supplemented by explicit activities to encourage parental reflection.

EXPLICIT RELATIONSHIP-BUILDING ACTIVITIES

Specific activities are used to encourage couples to talk and listen to each other. For example, every group meeting ends with 'talk and listen' time when parents sit with their partner and take turns to talk and listen for five minutes each about some aspect of the session such as 'what their hopes and fears' are for their baby. The discussion topic is less important than the communication skills practice, and over different sessions, parents are introduced to reflective listening and effective ways of conflict resolution. Facilitators generally find initially setting up 'talk and listen' time within the group quite challenging until parents understand the rationale and try out the activity. Parents' comments from the qualitative evaluation (Hogg *et al.* 2015) indicate that they have valued participating and 82 per cent felt their relationship with their partner had improved. They talked about how Baby Steps had taught them new ways to communicate:

> The course taught me how to talk to my partner, and the 'Talk and Listen' worksheet that they gave us really helped with that. It's hard, because he works a lot so we don't have time to talk much, but since the course we sit down now when he gets home for an hour, and we talk about our days and how the baby has been and about any worries, and listen to each other. It's a new way of discussing. Before, he used to just come home and spend the evening on the laptop. It has improved our relationship. (Mum – experiencing social isolation)

Parents also said that they had learnt how to manage disagreements by staying calm, taking a break if they were feeling stressed and then 'actively listening' to what their partner was saying:

> We communicate much better now, based on what I learnt in the session about how to manage disagreements. We used to not talk and second-guess what each other was feeling, but now we try to take five, stay calm and really listen to each other. (Mum – young parent)

Parents made links between discussing what music unborn babies responded to with an awareness that negative sounds could also have an impact:

You don't realize even, you don't have to be fighting, but just shouting, how much shouting can affect the baby. (Dad – involvement with children's services).

Results from the pre- and post-measures study (Brookes, Coster and Sanger 2015) confirmed that parents' relationship satisfaction significantly improved during the antenatal phase of the programme. Although some parents identified 'talk and listen' time's impact on their relationship skills, it is highly likely that they were influenced by the wider implicit ethos of Baby Steps alongside the more explicit activities.

CONCLUSION

Babies are born socially interactive with an innate desire to connect with others, and the way in which their psychological, emotional and social development unfolds is largely dependent upon the nature of the relationships in which they participate. While many will develop within the context of loving, attuned relationships, others may experience insensitivity, which impacts on the way their brain wires, emotion and behaviour are regulated and the security of their attachment (Schore and Schore 1999).

The transition to parenthood is a challenging time for all new parents and those with extra support needs can come from across the socio-economic spectrum. There is a strong economic case for early intervention rather than later treatment when adversities have already impacted on health and development (Heckman 2008).

NSPCC's investment in developing and evaluating this perinatal programme (Hogg *et al.* 2015) has significantly shifted the balance to include emotional health alongside physical health.

The Baby Steps programme is grounded in theoretical and research evidence about the transition to parenthood and aims to enable expectant parents to take a reflective stance (Underdown 2013) about how best to support their partner relationship and the relationship with their developing baby. Each part of the programme is essential, from the initial home visit, to the planning, preparation and supervision time, the implicit modelling and the explicit activities. As Aristotle is famously quoted as saying, 'The whole is greater than the sum of the parts.'

REFERENCES

Benoit, D., Parker, K.C.H. and Zeanah, C.H. (1997) 'Mothers' representations of their infants assessed prenatally: stability and association with infants' attachment classifications.' *Journal of Child Psychology and Psychiatry 38*, 3, 307–313.

Brookes, H., Coster, D. and Sanger, C. (2015) *Evaluation of the Baby Steps Programme: Pre- and Post-Measures Study – Large Type*. London: NSPCC.

Heckman, J.J. (2008) 'The Case for Investing in Disadvantaged Young Children.' In First Focus (ed.) *Big Ideas for Children: Investing in Our Nation's Future*. Washington, D.C.: First Focus. Available at: http://heckmanequation.org/content/resource/case-investing-disadvantaged-young-children (Accessed: 7 December 2016).

Hogg, S., Coster, D. and Brookes, H. (2015) *Baby steps: Evidence from a relationships-based perinatal education programme – summary document*. Available at: https://www.nspcc.org.uk/globalassets/documents/research-reports/baby-steps-evidence-relationships-based-perinatal-education-programme.pdf (Accessed: 2 November 2016).

Kennedy, H., Landor, M. and Todd, L. (eds) (2011) *Video Interaction Guidance: A Relationship-Based Intervention to Promote Attunement, Empathy and Wellbeing*. Philadelphia: Jessica Kingsley Publishers.

Schore, A.N. and Schore, S. (1999) *Affect Regulation and the Origin of the Self: The Neurobiology of Emotional Development*. Hillsdale, NJ: Lawrence Erlbaum Associates.

Schrader McMillan, A., Barlow, J. and Redshaw, M. (2009) *Birth and Beyond: A Review of the Evidence About Antenatal Education*. University of Warwick/University of Oxford. Available at: http://217.35.77.12/research/england/health/dh_109830.pdf (Accessed: 21 December 2016).

Stern, D.N. (1995) *The Motherhood Constellation: A Unified View of Parent-Infant Psychotherapy*. London: Karnac Books.

Underdown, A. (1998a) 'Investigating techniques used in parenting classes.' *Health Visitor 71*, 2, 65–68.

Underdown, A. (1998b) 'The transition to parenthood.' *British Journal of Midwifery 6*, 8, 508–511.

Underdown, A. (2013) 'Parent-infant relationships: supporting parents to adopt a reflective stance.' *Journal of Health Visiting 1*, 2, 76–79.

CHAPTER 13

Lullaby Africa

Using Indigenous Songs, Massage, Psycho-Education and Play
to Develop Baby Bonding in Groups of Traumatized Parents

Caroline Feltham-King and Rachel Moody

We describe attachment-enhancing 'baby bonding' groups for mothers
and babies living in extreme deprivation in sub-Saharan Africa. The
work was piloted in 2011 by two British play therapists, Helen Howes
and Debi Maskell-Graham, and has grown into Lullaby Africa, a
registered charity promoting secure attachment between parents
and children. We include reflections on working cross-culturally,
participants' comments and descriptions of *moments of vitality* creating
positive change for both parents and babies.

LULLABY AFRICA'S CULTURAL CONTEXT

Lullaby Africa began in Kisumu, Kenya's third-largest city, and has
extended to Kisoro in Uganda. In Kisumu's densely populated peri-
urban settlements, there is no easy access to water, sanitation or health
care and families live a hand-to-mouth existence. Though fertile, the

area surrounding Kisoro is very poor, so malnutrition is common and few girls complete primary education.

In such challenging environments, pregnancy for many women is not a time of excited anticipation. Instead, HIV/AIDS is a harsh reality, rape, prostitution and transactional sex are commonplace, and maternal and infant mortality rates are shockingly high. Frequent domestic and community violence further increases the likelihood of maternal depression (Cooper *et al.* 2009). These factors, along with the hyper-vigilance and dissociation resulting from interpersonal trauma, make it hard for mothers to provide sensitive care and emotional security for children (Van der Kolk 2014; WHO 2004). This heightens the risk of passing trauma and disorganized attachment patterns on to the next generation (de Zuluetta 2006).

Although mothers carry infants tied to their backs, co-sleep and breastfeed on demand, once they can sit unsupported, babies may be left alone for hours while their mothers fetch water, visit the market or work long shifts. The women are unaware that these separations are frightening and unsafe for babies. Strict discipline is believed to instil character, so the norm is for parents to chastise their children verbally and physically. In Uganda, babies are beaten when they do not settle to sleep.

WORKING CROSS-CULTURALLY

Lullaby Africa respects local cultural child-rearing practices, but challenges those that are incongruent with attachment security. We seek to do this in a facilitative rather than critical way. For example, we encourage mothers to take their babies with them when possible, or to find a neighbour to mind them.

We value discussions with our interpreters and community representatives, to understand the linguistic and cultural context of their communities, as they are so different from our usual working environments. For example, in Luo (Kisumu's main language), the word for 'baby' applies up to about nine months of age. After this, the word for 'child' is used. There is no linguistic distinction between a toddler, pre-school child or older child, nor is there any difference in parental expectations or responsibilities given.

Paired working in Africa enables peer supervision, essential in ensuring the facilitators reflect on difficult observations or conversations before deciding how best to respond, if at all. We seek to *be the message* so that workshops are a safe space for parents and babies, within which loving and intimate interactions may be created in the moment.

Making time to debrief after each session and share with Lullaby Africa trustees and supporters after trips protects us from experiencing secondary trauma as a result of seeing, hearing or imagining the traumatic experiences these mothers and babies endure (Cairns 2002).

THE BABY BONDING MODEL

British health and education professionals liaise with local leaders to run free workshops and establish informal baby bonding groups. Before each series of four workshops, community representatives, often accompanied by the British volunteers, visit homes to invite mothers to attend. Inviters explain that child sponsorship or financial assistance is not available, to clarify expectations. Signed permission is sought for the use of film and personal stories when explaining and evaluating Lullaby Africa's work, and names are changed for privacy.

The workshops teach parents to use gentle touch and to look lovingly at their babies while singing or talking to them. Through an attuned relationship, they can then build foundations for social understanding, empathy, language and cognitive development (Gerhardt 2014). We help mothers understand and develop their babies' capabilities using simple interactional games, and demonstrate how to comfort them when distressed, so that they start to see their baby as a unique person with their own thoughts, feelings and needs. Thus the quality of mother-baby relationships is improved through joyful, attuned experiences and enhanced **reflective functioning** (Cross and Kennedy 2011; Maskell-Graham 2016).

Regular follow-up visits consolidate the teaching, until some skilled participants feel confident to run workshops and groups independently. Lullaby Africa's model therefore empowers **baby bonding champions**.

BABY MASSAGE

Mothers are taught how to massage their babies gently, as a way of expressing love rather than simply to protect dry skin. Parents are also keen to hear about the potential health benefits of baby massage, as medical advice is expensive. Once each amenable baby is stripped and laid on their mother's lap, a facilitator pours some oil into every mother's palm. This giving and receiving in turn connects the group, creates calm and prepares parents to *tune in* to their babies.

Teaching is cumulative, adding new moves for different body parts in each session, modelled using soft-bodied black dolls. Mothers are invited to notice any preferences their baby might show. Consistent with research (Underdown, Norwood and Barlow 2013), we have observed previously unresponsive mothers becoming intrusive, in their eagerness to participate and *get it right*. So while one facilitator demonstrates, another guides those who handle their baby roughly and reassures others whose babies are avoiding their touch or gaze, helping them to wait for baby's initiative (Trevarthen 2011). When older babies resist lying down, mothers are advised to follow this initiative by massaging the child sitting supported in their lap.

A year after attending a workshop, Celine reflected on the impact of what she had learned, saying: 'The Baby Bonding Programme helped me, especially when my baby was sick in the hospital. I used to massage her, keep her to my heart, touch her slowly, slowly and I saw it made a quite big difference.'

LULLABIES

Across all cultures, lullabies are recognized as soothing when sung to babies, accompanied by intimate movements like cradling and stroking. They have similar melodies, tempos and rhythms and are a musical form of **parentese**. At six months, babies attend to their mother's singing even more than to their speech (Music 2014). Lullabies calm and connect parent and child (Baker and Mackinlay 2006; Maskell-Graham 2009).

Most mothers we meet do not sing or play at all with their young children, who are usually silent, unaffectionate and lacking curiosity. When asked to teach us their songs, few women can remember being sung to as a child. It seems that deprivation, displacement and depression have raided the treasury of songs that would have passed down the generations, along with ways of cherishing children. We have reintroduced indigenous songs in each language, to accompany the massage moves.

LOOKING AT BABY

Every group session starts by asking each mother how she is, and we help mothers name what their baby is doing in the moment and how they might be feeling. For example: 'My baby is sleeping; my baby is tired.' We then consider together what their babies may need from them, helping parents perceive and react appropriately to their child's signals.

After explaining the neuroscientific importance of giving loving looks to babies, we invite mothers to cradle their babies and gaze at them. This is a wondrous moment for many, as the babies hold eye contact, smile and even vocalize. Many parents have not previously realized that babies are sociable. For example, at just 13, Yolanda was the youngest mother Lullaby Africa had encountered. She had conceived through a forced encounter and left education. Already caring for her HIV-positive parents and younger siblings, she was deeply ashamed of her situation. Yolanda came to the workshop on the condition that a neighbour carried her daughter so that she was not seen in public with a baby.

Yolanda was reluctant to hold her daughter and when baby Florence was placed in her arms she stared at the ground, rather than at her four-month-old, whose eyes were searching her mother's face. At our suggestion, Yolanda glanced at her daughter and was startled by her gaze. With our encouragement, she made eye contact again and for the first time, looked deeply into her baby's eyes and was rewarded by a beautiful smile, which she shyly returned. In the following session, Yolanda and Florence discovered how to talk to each other and by the third session, Yolanda voluntarily placed Florence on her lap and smiled at her, ready to begin.

TALKING TO BABY

Mothers are generally surprised to learn that babies can hear them in utero. We teach that parentese is a universal way to speak to babies and that babies are born wanting to communicate (Trevarthen 2011). Parents do not realize that coos and babbling can be considered invitations to join their baby in conversation. Sarah accompanied a friend to one baby bonding session while pregnant and attended a subsequent workshop. Interviewed three years later, she said:

> Helen taught me how to speak with my child when he was still in the womb. I liked that and it has helped me so much to build that bond between me and my son. He is now active and loving. Thank you.

With such adversity, this shows that even a small amount of information can improve maternal wellbeing and mind-mindedness and help build good relationships from the start (Glover and Barlow 2014).

COMFORTING BABY

The teaching in the third session centres on how parents can be a safe presence by using loving touch, reassuring words and rhythmic movements to comfort their child in distress. Mothers learn how reliant babies are on a calmer adult to manage their stress, so as a group we practise cradling babies close to our hearts and rocking them while repeating, 'I am here; you are safe,' in the women's mother tongue. This helps calm the anxious mothers, so that they in turn may soothe their babies. To avoid reminding women of their own unresolved traumatic experiences, we illustrate the body's flight, fight or freeze responses through a humorous drama.

Parents are unaware of the long-term developmental damage caused by leaving babies in distress, or of being physically or emotionally hurt, especially by their caregivers. As they learn about this, some begin to question their parenting and move towards a more supportive, authoritative style (Baumrind 1993). For example, Joshua was the first man who attended our baby bonding sessions in 2013. We showed him how to hold his three-month-old daughter, smile and wait for her to make a sound, before copying her. Not expecting a baby to be communicative, he shed tears of joy at their first conversation. This moment of connection became a turning point; he and his wife Lucy learned to listen to their six older children, rather than discipline them harshly. As a couple, they now resolve their differences through discussion rather than fighting, and say their marriage is stronger and family life is happier. Now, Joshua and Lucy are strong advocates for baby bonding groups in their community, and Joshua teaches men to be loving and respectful husbands and fathers instead of abusive. Lucy said, 'Baby Bonding is a good teaching. It has helped me to care about my children, to talk to them, look in their face and to show them a good life.'

PLAYING WITH BABY

'It is possible to play with a baby,' remembered Ruth from a baby bonding session she attended out of curiosity with a friend. When we first met Ruth and Blessing (nine months old), they clearly knew how to have fun together, playing peek-a-boo and clapping along to their favourite songs. The following year we observed Blessing chatting and playing inquisitively, in stark contrast to many other toddlers. 'Now my child is bright!' exclaimed Ruth with pride.

We teach peek-a-boo, bringing delight to all. We show how older babies enjoy simple turn-taking exchanges, grasping and exploring an object, holding it out to an adult and then receiving it back again. This builds on the looking and listening taught in previous sessions, showing how **primary intersubjectivity** builds a good foundation for **secondary intersubjectivity** (Cross and Kennedy 2011). We model progressive object-related play: taking objects in and out of containers, stacking objects and then using them symbolically for pretend play.

On home visits, we have seen babies sucking pieces of metal, discarded pill packets and plastic bags near unconcerned adults as toys are unavailable. We demonstrate play using safe objects found in even the poorest homes: a cloth, cup, spoon and bowl. The atmosphere in the final session is very relaxed and full of laughter, as mothers and children play together.

ENDING

The group celebrates completing the course by singing traditional songs, with instruments made from readily available items. The final session ends with a presentation for each parent and baby – a certificate, a knitted teddy and a photograph of the dyad taken on the home visit or at the first session. Before leaving, participants are invited to continue meeting as a group or in local clusters, to encourage each other, to practise what they have learned, and to teach their friends and neighbours.

EMPOWERING PARENTS TO CHANGE COMMUNITIES

Mary had always sung to her children because her mother had sung to her; however, she also used to shout at them and beat them sometimes, too. Attending a workshop in 2011, she learned to be consistently kind to them, play with them and massage them. As Mary experienced the rewards of bonding with her own children, she started speaking to neighbours, discouraging them from shouting at their babies when they cried or could not feed, and showing them how to cradle, massage and calm them with singing. The following year, with two baby bonding friends, she began hospital visits, to comfort sick babies and share her knowledge with mothers and nursing staff. Then she ran a workshop for women and their babies in her family's village. She had become a baby bonding champion!

During sessions, parents are asked to share what they have learned with latecomers, giving us the opportunity to assess the level of understanding around the group, correct any points lost in translation and observe potential baby bonding champions. Lullaby Africa teams visit to develop baby bonding until local parents feel empowered to take the lead in sharing the messages independently of Western professionals.

Around Kisumu, there are now ten known baby bonding groups meeting through the year, led by baby bonding champions who signify their leadership by wearing Lullaby Africa T-shirts. Two large groups meet in Kisoro led by Ugandan volunteers, with one workshop specifically supporting young mothers who are sex workers. The hospital director in Goma, Democratic Republic of Congo has asked Lullaby Africa to develop a teaching model that can be shared through health professionals and village committees across their war-torn district.

CONCLUSION

This work is challenging as we touch on issues such as poverty, rape, domestic violence and corporal punishment. We are encouraged, however, by the observed effectiveness of assisting traumatized women to break cycles of emotional and cognitive deprivation, through developing connected interaction with their children. This short, simple, group parent education programme, using indigenous songs and baby massage, lessens the impact of multiple stresses for both mothers and babies. Moreover, its enabling approach equips parents to become agents of transformative change for their peers and communities.

REFERENCES

Baker, F. and Mackinlay, E. (2006) 'Sing, soothe and sleep: a lullaby education programme for first-time mothers.' *British Journal of Music Education 23*, 2, 147.

Baumrind, D. (1993) 'The average expectable environment is not good enough.' *Child Development 64*, 1299–1317.

Cairns, K. (2002) *Attachment, Trauma and Resilience: Therapeutic Caring for Children.* London: British Association for Adoption and Fostering (BAAF).

Cooper, P.G., Tomlinson, M., Swartz, L., Landman, M., Molteno, C., Stein, A., McPherson, K. and Murray, L. (2009) 'Improving quality of mother-infant relationship and infant attachment in socioeconomically deprived community in South Africa: randomised controlled trial.' *British Medical Journal 338*, 974.

Cross, J. and Kennedy, H. (2011) 'How and Why Does VIG Work?' In H. Kennedy, M. Landor and L. Todd (eds) (2011) *Video Interaction Guidance: A Relationship-Based Intervention to Promote Attunement, Empathy and Wellbeing.* Philadelphia: Jessica Kingsley Publishers.

de Zulueta, F. (2006) *From Pain to Violence: The Traumatic Roots of Destructiveness.* 2nd edn. Chichester: John Wiley & Sons.

Gerhardt, S. (2014) *Why Love Matters: How Affection Shapes a Baby's Brain.* 2nd edn. London: Routledge.

Glover, V. and Barlow, J. (2014) 'Psychological adversity in pregnancy: what works to improve outcomes?' *Journal of Children's Services 9*, 2, 96–108.

Maskell-Graham, D. (2009) *Baby Bonding: An Evaluation of Maternal Behaviours Associated with Secure Attachment.* Unpublished thesis. Canterbury Christ Church University.

Maskell-Graham, D. (2016) *Reflective Functioning and Play: Strengthening Attachment Relationships in Families from Pregnancy to Adolescence.* Nottingham: big toes little toes.

Music, G. (2014) *Nurturing Natures: Attachment and Children's Emotional, Sociocultural, and Brain Development.* Hove: Psychology Press.

Trevarthen, C. (2011) 'Confirming Companionship in Interests, Intentions and Emotions.' In H. Kennedy, M. Landor and L. Todd (eds) (2011) *Video Interaction Guidance: A Relationship-Based Intervention to Promote Attunement, Empathy and Wellbeing.* Philadelphia: Jessica Kingsley Publishers.

Underdown, A., Norwood, R. and Barlow, J. (2013) 'A realist evaluation of the processes and outcomes of infant massage programs.' *Infant Mental Health Journal 34*, 6, 483–495.

Van der Kolk, B.A. (2014) *The Body Keeps the Score: Brain, Mind, and Body in the Healing of Trauma*. London: Penguin Books.

World Health Organization (WHO) (2004) *The Importance of Caregiver-Child Interactions for the Survival and Healthy Development of Young Children: A Review*. Geneva: Department of Child and Adolescent Health and Development, World Health Organization.

Mellow Parenting

Help for Families with Exceptionally Difficult Circumstances
to Make the Best Relationships with Their Children

Christine Puckering with Rachel Tainsh and Lynnaire Doherty

In this chapter I describe Mellow Parenting, a psycho-educational nurturing programme, and give examples from working with families in Scotland, Tajikistan and New Zealand.

BACKGROUND

Mellow Parenting is a charity with its roots in Scotland but with national and international branches. It began with a group of mothers in a family centre in an economically deprived area of central Scotland, where a social worker with group experience, a psychologist with an interest in very early interaction and a child care worker combined their skills to produce a programme that supported parents as people, as well as tackling parenting issues directly. The major underlying principles of the groups came from attachment theory, but ideas from social learning, adult education and cognitive behavioural theory are also accessed.

FURTHER DEVELOPMENTS

Since its early days, the original Mellow programme has been evaluated and refined to include fathers as well as mothers, and additional programmes were created for babies under a year and antenatally, as the evidence of the importance of the first 1001 critical days became clearer (Leadsom *et al.* 2014; WAVE Trust with Department for Education 2013). Mellow Parenting groups remain committed to addressing social and health inequalities and delivering outcome-based programmes to all parents.

MELLOW GROUP FACILITATORS

Mellow Parenting groups are delivered across a range of settings by early years workers, such as health visitors and social workers. All workers must undergo the three-day 'Going Mellow' training, which equips them with all the manuals and materials as well as skills and knowledge they need to run a group. The manuals are a guide but not a prescription, and nurturance for parents and children and sensitivity to group process are key.

A DAY-LONG PROGRAMME

During the day, the parents and babies are together for lunchtimes and activities but babies are cared for in a babies' group for parts of the day to give parents time to talk and reflect. The personal group for parents targets depression, self-esteem and partner violence, among other topics. The direct work on parenting starts in the group, where parents, staff and babies share a lunchtime meal and have a chance to try messy play, simple cooking, songs and games and any activity that will encourage parent-baby interaction. These simple caregiving and playful activities are a chance for parents and babies to enjoy each other's company in ways they have not known before. Facilitators also make a ten-minute home video of each parent and baby during a mealtime and later give positive strengths-based feedback to help parents notice what works well.

GROUP FACILITATORS

The skill of the facilitator is in supporting the parents. The willingness to get alongside parents and babies is much more significant than academic qualifications. Anything that did not turn out as they would have wished can be taken to the group, who can generate their own suggestions. The role of the facilitator is not to solve problems, but to encourage the group in sharing problems and generating their own solutions.

THE SETTINGS

Mellow Parenting groups are run in a number of settings: children's centres, clinics, early years centres, social work agencies, and by statutory and voluntary sectors. Each setting is likely to have its own referral pathway but the tackling of the most complex problems – including parental mental ill health, previous child protection proceedings, domestic violence, parental learning disabilities and substance abuse – is often part of the picture.

OUTREACH

When a family is referred, the facilitator approaches them and makes a home visit. We do not send an appointment letter, which the parent may have difficulty reading. They may also not know the clinic or base or be too intimidated to attend. If parents fail to turn up for a group, a friendly phone call can lead to an offer of extra support to get to the group the next week, if needed. All Mellow materials are designed for parents with low literacy skills. Activities, videos and discussion are the main tools in the group, minimizing the demands on literacy that can exclude the very parents who need most help.

MELLOW BABIES SESSIONS

Mellow Babies for mothers or fathers runs for a full day a week for 14 weeks, involving the parent and baby. We do not mix mothers and fathers in the same group, as many of the issues discussed, including emotional and physical development, domestic violence or childhood abuse, are more easily discussed in single-gender groups, although some services run parenting workshops for parents together.

A TYPICAL DAY

A morning starts with the babies going to the baby group and breakfast for the parents, who may well have skipped their own needs to get the baby to the centre. The parents then have their group. There are 11 essential sessions and another 3 optional sessions, tailored to the needs of each group of parents.

Essential personal sessions conducted separately for mothers and fathers include: Introductions – we can work it out; Who am I? Trust; My family – then and now; Life stories; Being a dad for fathers/Self-esteem for mothers; You and your body; Pregnancy and birth; Child protection; The future; and Where are we now?

JOINT LUNCHTIME

Babies join staff and parents for a joint lunchtime, songs and finger games and an activity, which might be gentle massage, looking at picture books, making musical shakers or treasure baskets. The group plans an outing, which can introduce parents to local activities and resources for parents and babies, which are free or very inexpensive, and which they do not know about or do not have the confidence to access.

PSYCHO-EDUCATION

After lunch the babies return to the babies' group, while mothers and fathers take part in a parenting workshop based on their own home video and parenting topics. At the end of the day, the parents go away with a 'Have a Go' task to practise new ways to interact with their baby. This could be, for example, to assemble a treasure basket from simple objects in the house, park or garden.

PARENTS WITH COMPLEX PROBLEMS BENEFIT

The groups have been very successful in working with parents with complex problems, many beginning in their own childhood experiences (Puckering *et al.* 2010), who have themselves never received sensitive care. They often find it hard to know how to make attuned relationships with their babies, or to trust other adults. They may make poor choices in their romantic relationships, either being too trusting with the wrong people or too defended to allow themselves to make an enduring bond. In similar ways, they can be distrustful or too demanding of services.

ATTENDANCE

Most Mellow Parenting groups, planned to be for 6–8 parents, get about 80 per cent attendance and low attrition. Once parents sample the programme and feel supported, they want it to go on forever!

THE 'LIFE STORY' EXERCISE

This is one of the most challenging sessions, but pivotal in the life of the group and often for the individual. Parents are asked to draw or write the important positive or negative events in their lives, as a time line, which might be based on a river or pathway or even a spiral or a tree. They then take turns to tell the group as much or as little as they feel comfortable with. This session rarely passes without the shedding of some tears, and often the disclosure of traumatic past events.

Finding that they are not alone in their experience, for example of childhood sexual abuse or domestic violence, can be empowering and lead to the mother or father making changes in their lives. The issue of the safety of their own or other children has to be addressed if abusers are still likely to be active. The task of the facilitator is to keep the group safe, by providing boundaries, keeping the more talkative members on topic and drawing out quiet members, and calmly addressing risks, including child protection.

Parents regularly report that having a chance to think about themselves and the influences that formed them is not something they have done before. To be listened to without questions and interruptions and not judged is a precious experience. The power of the group, if skilfully managed by the facilitators, lies in the sharing and discovery that a mother or father is not alone. The role of the facilitator is not to solve a parent's problem but to use the group members to generate solutions. It may be that another parent has successfully managed the same issue in a different way. That parent receives endorsement of their skill. The recipient leaves with a new strategy to try. The group should finish their 14 weeks with an increased sense of confidence in their own parenting but also the knowledge that they can rely on other people to help them if they ask for it. I am humbled by the adversities some families have faced and survived.

The group environment is central to Mellow Babies. It generates its own solutions, with a consequent growth in parents' sense of self-efficacy (Bion 2014; Foulkes and Ledbetter 1969). Finding their own answers also ensures that they are culturally appropriate. The facilitators do not impose a particular model of parenting and only challenge when the group's proposals are contrary to what is known about the optimum outcomes for children. For example, physical chastisement is never endorsed.

Parents in New Zealand regularly expect their children to say *karakia* (grace) before eating. It is not the role of the group to endorse or reject this, but to help parents find a way to do this with the least stress for the babies, by, for example, not putting the tempting food in front of a hungry baby until *karakia* has been said.

In Russia, where poverty is rife, it is not culturally acceptable to play with food substances, so making multi-coloured spaghetti to explore with fingers has to be replaced with another parent-child activity such as coloured sand paintings.

Solutions are often very simple once the parent has had a chance to stand back and see the situation in a new light with the aid of their own video recording and the support of other parents. Other cultural variations can arise in what is acceptable in baby play activities and draw on facilitators' creativity and professional background.

CASE HISTORY – EDINBURGH

Maria, the mother of six-month-old baby John, had been sexually abused by her father as a child. Her firstborn had been removed and subsequently adopted. She was referred by the joint social work and health visiting team, who questioned whether she might have learning difficulties. John was on the child protection register.

Maria was first seen at her home, which she shared with her partner and his parents. She readily engaged with the programme and attended even when she felt unwell. She loved the video feedback and shared with pride her new awareness of how attentive she was to John during his lunchtime and how this might support his development. She was loyal and supportive to another mother, whose child was in foster care during the group.

At the end of the group John's name had been removed from the 'at risk' register and Maria was starting to look for a part-time job to support her family.

MELLOW PARENTING IN TAJIKISTAN

BACKGROUND

Tajikistan is one of the poorest countries in Central Asia. It gained independence from the Soviet Union in 1991, and a drawn-out civil war ended in 1997. The country faces major development challenges. It ranks 133 out of 187 countries on the 2014 United Nations Development Programme Human Development Index (UNDP 2014). Lack of economic opportunities and high levels of poverty have been particularly hard on women as, until recently, labour migration involved 90 per cent of the male population. With state benefits inadequate, many Tajik families have relied on cash remittances from household members currently living abroad. Poverty is a major cause of harm to children in Tajikistan.

When a family reaches crisis point, there are few community services to intervene. There is little help for the family to plan how to retain care of a child, rather than abandon them to an institutional care setting such as a 'Baby Home'. Mothers of disabled children are left alone without wider family support as a consequence of shame and stigma, and children with disabilities are often placed in orphanages.

REFERRAL ROUTE

HealthProm, an international nongovernmental organization (NGO) whose focus is to give vulnerable children the best start in life and prevent them entering institutional care, was the first organization to introduce Mellow Parenting to Tajikistan.

Training was delivered to 23 new Tajik Mellow Parenting facilitators in 2010 and 2013 followed by ongoing support. Family support centre teams identified mothers and children who might benefit. Eight Mellow Parenting groups at family support centres were delivered between 2010 and 2014.

The 14-week groups were attended by 68 mums and 68 children, and only 1 mother dropped out. Twenty-four mums were identified who wanted to place their children in a Baby Home, four of whom had a disability. Following the group, no child entered the Baby Home, one child already placed in the Baby Home was taken back home, one mother started her own business, three completed their schooling, two went to university and eight found jobs.

Five of the original facilitators have undertaken specialist training to facilitate Mellow Parenting programmes for families of children with autism. So far, 38 such families have benefitted from the Mellow Parenting programmes.

CASE HISTORY – TAJIKISTAN

Nazokat left her three children aged six months, three years and six years in a Baby Home and went to Russia to work. The children's grandmother visited the children twice a week and was invited to attend a Mellow Parenting group. A few weeks into the group, the grandmother phoned Nazokat in Russia and demanded that she return home. She explained that the children were suffering without their mother. Nazokat returned and the children are now back at home with her, continuing to be supported by the Mellow group and family support team.

Parents who have completed a Mellow programme have been empowered to fight for the rights of their children to be included in society and to attend school. Some are now working as group facilitators, while others were confident enough to seek and find employment. They have built up a circle of friends, and are invited to each other's houses and to social celebrations.

Parents reported that they are benefitting from sharing their feelings with peers and seeing their children become more independent and learning new skills.

MELLOW PARENTING IN NEW ZEALAND: MELLOW BABIES – HOKI KI TE RITO PARENTING PROGRAMME

Ohomairangi Trust is a Kaupapa Māori-run nonprofit NGO, based in South Auckland, New Zealand, and is delivered according to Māori principles. Hoki ki te Rito is a cultural adaptation of Mellow Parenting developed to match underlying Kaupapa Māori values. It is offered to families needing specialist support with their children that addresses physical, sensory, communication, socio-emotional, behavioural and developmental needs as well as parenting or parent education needs.

The local District Health Board sponsored the adaptation, a pilot and an extended study across two providers, and owing to promising results, continues to fund this programme from the addictions budget. The focus is on intensive support to families where there is relationship breakdown. The children may be under Child Youth and Family Services (CYFS) child protection with a plan to transition them back into the care of the parents, or there may be a threat to parents' retaining custody of their children, owing to care and protection issues or neglect.

The Hoki ki te Rito parenting programme aims to provide a positive experience for Māori whānau (families), the indigenous population of New Zealand that has endured colonization since the early 1800s. Māori continue to be over-represented in negative statistics with high unemployment, high rates of poverty, low academic achievement, high rates of incarceration and suicide (youth and maternal), and the list goes on. Referrals are received from parents themselves or other family members, alongside various government agencies and community services.

The Mellow groups worked with mothers, fathers and grandparents aged 15–59, with a variety of problems such as being a single parent, CYFS involvement, being a parent who themselves have been involved with CYFS, current domestic abuse, substance abuse, welfare dependency and housing problems.

Amiria and her nine-month-old son, Tane, had just moved from a residential hostel placement for mothers and children, where they had spent nine months. They were now living in a supported community of mothers and children as they moved towards full transition into the community. Three of Amiria's older children had been removed from her as a result of domestic violence and neglect.

Amiria wanted to make changes and build a secure and loving relationship with Tane. She now engaged with Mellow Babies enthusiastically – she was always on time, had saved for a vehicle and drove herself and Tane to the programme every week without fail.

She started tentatively, and her mealtime video, filmed while she was on our waiting list for the next course, showed a mother feeding her child while sitting on the couch, noticing few of Tane's attempts to engage with her – she was so intent on getting the food into him. Over time she relaxed, and within a month the videos showed how much they now enjoyed their time chatting to one another during the meal, smiling, looking at each other and brimming with positive affect and responsiveness. The improvements in the quality of their interactions were also obvious during the weekly play activities and could be tracked across the videos taken at the start of the group, at the end and then again at three months after the completion of the programme.

Amiria has said that hearing the others' stories helped her to not feel so alone in her struggle to keep Tane, and her confidence that she could build a relationship with a strong foundation grew.

Amiria was determined to keep custody of her son and asked to use the video series as evidence in court to show that change had actually happened. Dr Christine Puckering was asked by the court judge to further comment on the videos. The outcome was that Amiria did retain custody/guardianship of Tane, they moved to independent living in their community, and Amiria took Tane to the local early childhood centre where she then spent time as a mother helper.

SUPPORTING PARENTS TO NOTICE SUCCESSFUL MOMENTS OF INTERACTION

There are many opportunities across a day for parents to discover new things about their children, and vice versa. By looking at mealtime videos, parents were helped to see the positive aspects in their interactions with their children.

During a massage group session, while a mother was giving her baby a massage, her four-year-old son, seeing the basket of dolls nearby, went to select a doll, took it and settled down beside his mother. Without prompting, he carefully laid his doll on a towel and began 'his baby's' massage, gently rubbing the doll's arms, legs and tummy, glancing at his mother and smiling. Mother noticed and commented later that she planned to continue the *mirimiri* (massage times) at home and would include her son to teach him about gentle touching.

CONCLUSIONS

Running a Mellow Group requires an investment of time and resources. Staff and baby group workers' time needs to be freed to run such a long and intensive group, and room space and simple catering are needed to make the group welcoming for parents who get few 'treats' in their lives. Continuity of facilitators is desirable to safeguard the integrity of the group process. Where managers understand that early investment pays off in the longer term, such investment is seen as wise. Too easily, through lack of understanding, resources are cut, staff time is trimmed and group process undermined. This is worthwhile but challenging work. It cannot be done 'on the cheap' and cutting resources may risk failing to achieve the best outcomes. Mellow Parenting gives free reflective consultation (supervision) for all facilitators after training for as long as they are running Mellow Groups, because of a belief that good supervision is necessary to help facilitators deliver the programme effectively and to support them in doing that.

Mellow Parenting methods have been used across the UK and across a variety of cultures. Working with families in the most challenging of circumstances and seeing the changes they make, and their becoming empowered, is both rewarding and humbling. This is not easy work and demands an investment from services but also a personal investment from facilitators.

REFERENCES

Bion, W.R. (2014) *Experiences in Groups, and Other Papers*. London: Routledge.

Foulkes, S.H. and Ledbetter, V. (1969) 'Note on transference in groups.' *Group Analysis 1*, 3, 135–146.

Leadsom, A., Field, F., Burstow, P. and Lucas, C. (2014) *The 1001 Critical Days: The Importance of the Conception to Age Two Period*. Available at: http://www.andrealeadsom.com/downloads/1001cdmanifesto.pdf (Accessed: 1 December 2016).

Puckering, C., McIntosh, E., Hickey, A. and Longford, J. (2010) 'Mellow Babies: a group intervention for infants and mothers experiencing postnatal depression.' *Counselling Psychology Review 25*, 1, 28–40.

United Nations Development Programme (UNDP) (2014) *Human Development Report 2014*. Available at: http://hdr.undp.org/en/composite/HDI (Accessed: 21 December 2016).

WAVE Trust in collaboration with Department for Education (2013) *Conception to Age 2 – The Age of Opportunity. Addendum to the Government's Vision for the Foundation Years: 'Supporting Families in the Foundation Years'*. Available at: http://www.wavetrust.org/our-work/publications/reports/conception-age-2-age-opportunity (Accessed: 1 December 2016).

REFLECTIVE PRACTICE

CHAPTER 15

Strong Bonds to Hold the Cradle

The Supervision Group as a Safe Space to Share
for Facilitators of Parent and Baby Groups

Margaret Gallop

The following is my experience of supervising a group of facilitators who were running mother and baby groups, including Baby Massage, Baby Watching and Watch, Wait and Wonder, as part of a set of postnatal interventions in children's centres, where concern had been expressed about bonding. The facilitators were parent infant therapists. The supervision group offered a **secure base** where the facilitators could describe their work, support each other, pool knowledge and ask for help with concerns and their moment-to-moment decision making. As trusting relationships developed, the supervision group became a valued resource, where the members were able to share the emotional impact the work had on them personally, without shame and embarrassment. They became more playful, using stories and imagery, and so became more flexible, adept and resourceful. Reflections are based on insights co-constructed with supervision group members.

THE IMPORTANCE OF ATTACHMENT
AND LEARNING FROM RESEARCH

Studies of child-rearing in humans and other mammals (Schore 2012) have highlighted the importance of attachment. Babies develop a secure attachment bond to their caregivers if the caregivers are attuned to them and understand their communications (Bowlby 1988). A similar experience of secure attachment can be created in the supervision groups (Driver 2005).

Research into wild African elephants has shown that where there is no support from other elephants, also known as 'allomothers', young mother elephants can fail in their mothering or reject their babies (Lee 1987). In human societies, mothers also need support and, in the absence of a helpful extended family, have to find a network of support in the locality.

Just as the mothers benefit greatly from mother and baby groups, so do the group facilitators benefit from support: sharing concerns, insights and experiences in a supervision group. To work well in their mother baby groups, the facilitators need to be able to attune to the real babies, attune to the baby feelings aroused in the mothers, as well as their own baby feelings, and keep hold of their grown-up thinking.

THE SUPERVISION GROUP AS A SECURE BASE

The supervision group can become a secure base for the facilitators (Holmes 2001), where group members can feel free to share their thoughts and feelings, negative as well as positive, and to be spontaneous and playful. To be able to notice, feel and put into words ambivalent feelings about the work is pivotal. It allows facilitators to help the mothers with their mixed feelings of love and hate for their babies.

REFLECTION

The therapist needs to feel held securely yet in a way that allows fluidity of movement, much as a parent has to feel secure in themselves with a flexibility of mind to respond to the baby and the environment. To provide a secure base, I, the supervisor, hold in mind the mothers and babies and the relationship between them, the **dynamic administration** of the supervision group, the facilitators, the organization, the supervision group process, and my own experience and responses. This is described as the **clinical hexagon** in supervision (Plant and Smith 2012).

THE GROUP AS A MEDIUM FOR SUPERVISION

The following example shows how valuable it is to have many eyes on the work, providing a multi-perspective view (Behr and Hearst 2005).

Padma, a facilitator, wanted to talk about a baby who seemed flat and not interested in what was going on around him. He did not search for his mother's face and she seemed not to notice his passivity. Padma was concerned and did not know where to start. The group discussed this animatedly, bringing in their varying professional experience. There was a query whether there could be something physically wrong with the baby. Padma then recounted that the mother had experienced a traumatic birth, with subsequent separation from her baby. The group agreed that the traumatic birth, medical treatment and separation had affected the mother and baby dyad and both of them needed restoring to full emotional as well as physical health. Padma was then clearer about her task.

REFLECTION

The facilitators' diverse work experiences with babies in different contexts added varying perspectives, so together they found a helpful way of thinking about the mother and baby.

THE PURPOSE OF SUPERVISION

Supervision is a vital aspect of therapy, like tidying a sewing box, separating tangled threads so you can find what you want in it next time you need it. As facilitators discuss their groups, they realize that they are not alone in their feelings. Often they understand their own reactions better when they see them mirrored in other people, and thereafter can claim them as their own (Foulkes and Anthony 1989). The supervision group members are learning all the time from each other, discussing ethical and risk issues and so increasing their professional expertise. They may also feel healed and restored by the understanding and comradeship of their co-workers.

The different functions of supervision have been described as the normative, formative and restorative functions of the supervision group (Inskipp and Proctor 1993). The normative function includes accountability, ethical considerations and evaluation. The formative function covers the educational aspects of supervision and the professional development of the practitioner. The restorative function describes the supportive process taking care of the health and wellbeing of the practitioner while working with stress and distress.

SETTING AND BOUNDARIES

The group had a pleasant setting, which helped everyone, including myself, to feel valued. We agreed on time boundaries and a regular rhythm of meeting. At one point when reorganizing my work schedule, I offered greater flexibility in the times I would be available. Instead of this being helpful, I found it had a confusing effect on the group. I learned that like a mother establishing sleeping and waking patterns, it was better to stick to existing rhythms and offer narrower choices (Langs and Dorpat 1994). With clear boundaries, any crossing of boundaries, like lateness, could become a visible non-verbal communication, whose symbolic meaning may be worth exploring (Foulkes 1984).

CONFIDENTIALITY BOUNDARIES WITHIN THE ORGANIZATION

I met regularly with the manager of the organization, which was important to raise issues which may be impeding good work, but a boundary was established that I would not pass on any private information shared in the group. The relationship of the supervision group to the organization is like the yolk in an egg, firmly held but with some flexibility, a container contained (Bion 1975).

THE SIZE OF THE GROUP

At times there could be pressure to include more members in the supervision group, which could arouse feelings of envy and competition. Group members felt more secure when they had a sense of agency and were consulted. I met new members individually prior to their joining the group, and discussed new arrivals in the group before they came. A new group member can stir up those early feelings of sibling rivalry, like a new baby joining the family. The optimal size of the group was three to four, but some facilitators preferred to meet me as a dyad, reflecting their dyadic mother and baby work. Each facilitator was working with a high number of mothers and babies and it was important to have time for considering a particular dyad as well as to keep an overview of each group.

CONTAINMENT AND THINKING

The facilitators were holding and containing strong feelings from the mother and baby groups (James 1994). They themselves became an outer container like a vacuum flask, which holds and protects the precious canister inside. They then needed somewhere to bring these confused or distressing feelings to share and explore. The secure base of the supervision group meant it was safe to put these feelings into words (Holmes 2001).

REFLECTION

When the mother was not emotionally available and able to contain her baby's feelings, the facilitator was the one who was strongly affected. The supervision group helped her to disentangle and understand these raw feelings, with the other group members supporting the process of thinking with an adult mind.

STRUCTURE WITHIN THE SESSION

It was helpful to establish a structure for the 90-minute-long session. Facilitators requested time slots, saying a little about what they wanted to talk about and what kind of response they might need. We would then agree an order and members would take it in turns to explain what they had brought to discuss. One facilitator may want ideas about setting up a group in a new venue, another may want to report on an assessment interview and another may want to report on a recent group session or think about what further help may be available for a mother who is causing concern. There is a tension for the facilitators between wanting their own turn to share and the opportunity to learn from others' experience.

RESONANCE WITHIN THE SUPERVISION PROCESS

My role as supervisor was to help each member present her work without interruption, unless there was something which needed clarification. The group would then discuss what the member had brought, which could include any thoughts, feelings and associations. There could be some playful suggestions or interactions. This developed a quality of heightened attention as facilitators resonated to the material like musical instruments tuning in to what was described (Foulkes 1977). Over time they felt more confident in sharing their spontaneous responses. The group then reflected on ideas that had been generated, and identified any new thinking to help understand the mothers and babies and their interactions and to make suggestions.

The following is an example of a diverse group providing life as well as work experience, giving multiple perspectives. Facilitators used free-flowing thoughts, associations and **resonance** in the supervision group, which enriched their discussion.

Kate, a facilitator, said she had felt uncomfortable about a socially isolated mother she had assessed for her baby massage group. This mother had finally become pregnant after fertility treatment. Early in the pregnancy, she had fallen down the stairs. During the interview, the baby had stayed asleep in their colour-coordinated pushchair, which also matched the mother's clothes. Kate wanted to work out why she felt anxious about this mother.

The supervision group included Helen, a new grandmother; Inge, who had not been able to have babies; and Joan, whose three children were just leaving home. Helen felt protective of the mother whom she felt needed support in her mothering. Inge remembered her painful feelings about infertility and Joan felt the distance between this young woman and her family. There was quite a bleak feeling in the room. The mother's world felt empty apart from the baby, who had hardly been mentioned and had slept throughout the assessment.

Helen noticed that the mother was keeping everything coordinated, as if she was afraid of feeling out of control. Inge wondered whether she was still in shock, as if she had never truly expected a real baby to come. 'Or is she afraid of her baby,' Helen wondered, 'the responsibility for another life?' Joan felt nervous about the fall down the stairs early in the pregnancy and reminded us that this had been a traditional way of trying to end a pregnancy. Inge playfully remembered the traditional rhyme about Jill (the mother's name) tumbling down the hill and spilling her bucket of water. After this there was an intense sadness in the room, then a sense of guilt and shock at having laughed about something that represented the loss of a baby. Kate reflected that there had been a flash of anger during the assessment interview from the mother, when Kate had asked about the baby. Inge wondered whether this mother would be able to come regularly to the group or if she would be an early drop-out.

Kate shared that talking about her client 'had clarified the powerful ambivalence this mother felt about her baby who, even though longed for, also aroused resentment. It was as though the baby had not quite arrived yet in her mind.' We realized that we had not even heard what gender the baby was. Kate decided then to pay particular attention to this mother, and if possible help her articulate her maternal ambivalence, which many parents experience, and so help this mother stay in the group and not fall away.

REFLECTION

A roller coaster ride of feelings can be aroused in the supervision process, all of which can give clues to the mother's feelings. Supervision can function like a microscope and provide greater clarity. Working with struggling mothers can bring up feelings that have been tucked away, because they are disturbing or distressing, like Inge's feelings about her own infertility.

Listening to each other in the supervision group, resonating to each other's experience and realizing you are not alone in having a strong reaction can be a relief and help with understanding the mothers' feelings. In this case the facilitators knew each other well and were able to accept and support each other. Maturity and adult thinking were needed to be able to notice, tolerate and express some of these difficult feelings.

Kate said, 'I found the mother's hostile feelings to her baby difficult. By discussing them in the supervision group I learned more about the mother and could become more empathic.'

REGULATION OF FEELINGS IN THE FACILITATORS

'Primary maternal preoccupation', a concept coined by Winnicott (1988), is the heightened sense of responsibility and involvement a mother feels with her new baby. A group can arouse similar feelings in a facilitator, as does the *carrying* of a supervision group (Doron 2013). Just as a mother learns to regulate her baby's feelings by soothing distress and being playful when baby needs stimulation, so facilitators resonate to the feelings expressed in their mother baby groups. Often these are non-verbal and first registered in the body, sensing what is happening in others, before it is translated into words by the mind (Schore 2012).

REFLECTION

When supervision group members helped regulate each other's feelings, and reduce the anxiety of the presenter, the groups started to feel closer, more intimate and effective.

AMBIVALENT FEELINGS ABOUT THE SUPERVISION GROUP

New facilitators may be anxious about joining an established supervision group, fearing exposure or embarrassment. For different reasons, experienced workers may feel the same. When the supervision group provides a place where both the new and the more experienced facilitators can continue to learn and refine their understanding without loss of face, professional collaboration broadens everyone's experience.

As the group grows in confidence, feelings of competition and rivalry (Gautier 2009), which may reflect similar dynamics among the mothers, can be explored (Kutter 1993).

A SECURE BASE ALLOWS FOR PLAY AND CREATIVITY

Play is an important step to creativity and using your whole self (Winnicott 1971). Supervision can be described as 'serious play' (Rosenblum 2004). The feedback from Kate, the facilitator, stated that:

> at its best supervision felt like a dance, with a sense of flow, delight, and connectedness, reflecting the fullness of life. When we felt free enough to play together, we could then help the mothers to find a more playful approach to their babies.

EXAMPLE

A facilitator, Jasmin, told us that a little boy was crying very hard when his mother put him down. It was as if he felt he had been dropped. Another group member suggested that he reminded her of Humpty Dumpty, that no one would ever be able to put 'back together again'.

There was a feeling of relief because, unlike a cracked egg, the little boy could be gathered back together, held and comforted.

REFLECTION
The playful space in the supervision group promoted attuned relationships between group members and encouraged moments of insight. Kate said, 'The support of the supervision group and its faith in my potential helped me to develop my professional confidence, so that I could enable the mothers to connect to their babies in more helpful ways.'

CONCLUSION
By bringing the painful feelings that mothers and babies aroused to the supervision group, the facilitators could think about them, rather than feeling frustrated or paralysed. This enabled them to conduct a different conversation with the mothers, which in turn changed the mothers' relationships with their babies.

At times of emotional and situational upheaval, the supervision group functioned like an anchor, developing strong bonds and a secure base, safe for sharing, considered decision making and promoting professional development. It also provided emotional support and healing for group facilitators running mother and baby groups.

At its best the supervision group becomes an attuned, resonant instrument for understanding the parents and babies and so contributes to the development of facilitators' professional confidence and good work in the organization.

REFERENCES
Behr, H. and Hearst, L. (2005) *Group Analytic Psychotherapy in Practice: Meeting of Minds*. Philadelphia: Whurr.

Bion, W.R. (1975) *Attention and Interpretation: A Scientific Approach to Insight in Psycho-analysis and Groups*. London: Tavistock.

Bowlby, J. (1988) *A Secure Base: Parent-Child Attachment and Healthy Human Development*. London: Routledge.

Doron, Y. (2013) 'Primary maternal preoccupation in the group analytic group.' *Group Analysis 47*, 1, 17–29.

Driver, C. (2005) 'Attachment and the Supervisory Alliance.' In C. Driver and E. Martin (eds) *Supervision and the Analytic Attitude*. London: Whurr.

Foulkes, S.H. (1977) 'Notes on the Concept of Resonance.' In L.R. Wolberg and M.L. Aronson (eds) *Group Therapy, 1977: An Overview*. New York: Stratton.

Foulkes, S.H. (1984) *Therapeutic Group Analysis*. London: Maresfield Reprints.

Foulkes, S.H. and Anthony, E.J. (1989) *Group Psychotherapy: The Psychoanalytic Approach*. 2nd edn. London: Karnac Books.

Gautier, D. (2009) 'The impact of sibling rivalry in group supervision.' *The Journal of the British Association for Psychoanalytic & Psychodynamic Supervision 1*, 6–8.

Holmes, J. (2001) *The Search for the Secure Base: Attachment Theory and Psychotherapy*. Hove: Brunner-Routledge.

Inskipp, F. and Proctor, B. (1993) *The Art, Craft and Tasks of Counselling Supervision: Professional Development for Counsellors, Psychotherapists, Supervisors and Trainees: Part 1: Making the Most of Supervision*. 2nd edn. Twickenham: Cascade Publications.

James, D.C. (1994) '"Holding" and "Containing" in the Group and Society.' In D. Brown and L. Zinkin (eds) *The Psyche and the Social World: Developments in Group-Analytic Theory*. London: Routledge.

Kutter, P. (1993) 'Direct and indirect ("reversed") mirror phenomena in group supervision.' *Group Analysis 26*, 2, 177–181.

Langs, R.J. and Dorpat, T. (1994) *Doing Supervision and Being Supervised: Supervision of Psychotherapy in Light of the Evolution and Architecture of the Human Mind*. London: Karnac Books.

Lee, P.C. (1987) 'Allomothering among African elephants.' *Animal Behaviour 35*, 1, 278–291.

Plant, R. and Smith, M. (2012) 'Group supervision: moving in a new range of experience.' *The Psychotherapist 50*, 2, 14–15.

Rosenblum, S. (2004) Review of *Supervising and Being Supervised: A Practice in Search of a Theory*, edited by Jan Wiener, Richard Mizen and Jenny Duckham. *Journal of the American Psychoanalytic Association 52*, 4, 1275–1279.

Schore, A.N. (2012) *The Science of the Art of Psychotherapy*. New York: W.W. Norton.

Winnicott, D.W. (1971) *Playing and Reality*. London: Tavistock.

Winnicott, D. (1988) *Babies and Their Mothers*. London: Free Association Books.

CHAPTER 16

Holding onto Hope – Engagement, Reflection and Attunement

Supporting Inner City Frontline Staff to Facilitate
a Young Parent and Baby Group

Tamara Hussain and Moira McCutcheon

This chapter describes the use of the reflective method to support
staff teams who ran parent-baby groups in a multi-cultural inner city
London borough; a public health initiative to engage vulnerable young
mothers and babies, who experienced multiple intergenerational and
complex problems. The team were play workers with a background
in early years, and many had grown up in the local communities
themselves. They aimed to encourage families to improve their health
and relationships, and to access social and employment opportunities.

The reflective method (Schon 1983) helped practitioners to provide
a containing space for parents and babies, once they had started to
gain insight into the emotional needs of the young mothers. Selma
Fraiberg's understanding that we need to hear the cry of the mother to
enable her to hear the cry of her baby (Fraiberg, Adelson and Shapiro
1975) provides our theoretical framework.

AIMS

The aims of the mother baby group were to improve parenting skills, to provide children with opportunities to engage in meaningful play and to develop positive relationships. Over time it transpired, in the reflective staff sessions, that many mothers suffered from a traumatic birth and depression and needed help to process these experiences (Parker 2015). This became an additional focus for the parent-baby groups.

Sessions were held in a welcoming space with toys, and offering opportunities for sand, water and messy play. Parents were encouraged to physically be on their baby's level. Space was found for one-to-one conversations with staff, to allow opportunities for confidential discussions when needed. The babies' ages ranged from a few months up to the age of two years.

BONDING AND BOUNDARIES

Activities in the mother baby group included baby massage (physically helping the bonding and healing process), reading stories or singing and listening to music, to encourage learning about their individual relationship and focusing on the aspects of motherhood that they enjoyed.

It could often be tempting for professionals to step into the maternal role, by taking the baby from the mother's arms and begin to offer a nurturing experience. This may be helpful in term of modelling positive interactions; however, it may inadvertently usurp the mother's position and leave her feeling inadequate: if baby responds to the professional, she may feel replaced, because she is not 'good enough' (Bell and Morse 2005).

Facilitators of the mother baby groups recognized that their role was to support mothers to build their relationship with their babies, and to take pleasure in watching them grow and change. They were able to model positive interactions with the baby, compliment the mother and notice the way in which the baby responded to her, to reinforce the notion of her being capable and everything her baby needed.

Genuinely felt praise could be transformative for the mothers. Having another person notice the close connection whilst acknowledging difficulties can feel rewarding and offer validation when a mother is feeling unsure about her own competency and ability to meet her baby's needs.

IMPACT OF GROUP SIZE

As the group grew in size, facilitators felt it to be loud and difficult to contain; the young parents were seen like a gang, slouching together chatting, paying little attention to their children; eyeing staff disdainfully when it was suggested that they might join in. Facilitators felt exhausted trying to build relationships with a large number of mothers. They felt despondent that the task was unmanageable and change impossible.

Once this was recognized, more intimate groups were established (of six to eight dyads maximum), where the individual needs of each mother and her child could be thought about and both held in mind. If they missed a session, their absence was followed up with a text message or phone call. The smaller size made it possible to tune into the specific needs of families, also avoiding children at risk slipping through the net.

THE REFLECTIVE METHOD

This approach recognizes the *emotional impact of the work* on the facilitators, who may defend against the pain of witnessing insensitive parenting by distancing themselves as having *seen it all before* and having *worse* families on their books (Brookfield 1998). At a debriefing time, as well as covering practical and safeguarding issues, discussions reflected on individuals, mothers and their children, and crucially, facilitators' own responses to them (Johns and Burnie 2013).

The opportunity to reflect each week in a safe and honest space allowed the facilitators to become vulnerable and to think about their own emotional responses. Support from colleagues in considering their own reactions to their clients allowed them to soften their, sometimes harsh, response to the parents' unsuitable behaviour, once they considered parents' painful experiences. As a result the staff team was able to access parents whom they had previously felt to be closed off to.

RECOGNIZING THE COMPETING NEEDS OF PARENT AND CHILD

When Bonnie, a small, quiet two-year-old, wanted to join in with her mother Stacey's art work, the mother screeched, 'This is mine; you're going to spoil it. Go away!'

On reflection, the team recognized that they found this painful to witness. They were then able to think about Stacey, being just 17, and understood that her immature competition with her small daughter was like the expression of a deprived toddler rather than a parent, because her needs had never been met either. In discussion, we could reflect on how babies' desire for attention, satisfaction and love could prompt mothers to feel resentful and envious, and that their own unmet desire for play, attention and space could compete with the needs of their babies.

Stacey's emotional hunger was impacting the whole group; the atmosphere felt competitive and tense. After reflecting on this, facilitators asked Stacey to volunteer in the group; an opportunity she relished. Once she was more secure in that her presence was valued, she started to soften her responses to her daughter, allowing her to be playful too.

MATERNAL AVAILABILITY – 'RUNNING ON EMPTY'

Sadia was 19 and living with six-month-old Ayaan in a dingy temporary flat plagued with pest infestation, damp and mould. They attended the group sporadically. Ayaan's delivery had been difficult and Sadia had struggled to bond with him. With little support from his father or the wider family, Sadia found it hard to manage Ayaan's poor health. They both seemed to be constantly unwell with minor coughs and colds.

Sadia would sit apart from Ayaan during the sessions, propping him up with cushions, placing blankets under his bottle to feed himself. 'He won't leave me alone,' she would often grumble, eyeing him distastefully. When facilitators coaxed her to join in with singing time or sit together in the baby corner, she would reply despairingly, 'I come here to have a break. I'm too tired to play with him.' This mother was experiencing postnatal depression and scant support; she had limited emotional resources and capacity to think about her baby's needs. This situation felt bleak and oppressive to the facilitators running the group.

REFLECTION

Just as Sadia struggled to keep Ayaan in her focus, the facilitators struggled to connect to Sadia. Some found Sadia miserable and 'impossible' to talk to. Others even forgot to remember her in the debriefing sessions even though concerns were raised about her lack of interest in her baby. Sadia and Ayaan's ongoing health difficulties were related not just to their poor living environment but also to the dysfunctional relationship that had developed between them. Sadia felt overwhelmed by her baby's needs and perceived Ayaan as a *selfish* baby; a parasite, consuming her energy. This prompted facilitators to experience her as uncaring, and they found it hard to think about her at all. It was also difficult for facilitators to develop a relationship with baby Ayaan, who did not make eye contact and generally had an impassive, expressionless gaze.

Once facilitators reflected how Ayaan's birth had left his mother with real physical injuries, which she associated with her baby, they were able to become more sympathetic and thoughtful of her difficulties in forming a relationship with him. Parent infant therapy was considered to be appropriate, as thinking about baby Ayaan was particularly difficult when mother Sadia was distressed or preoccupied with practical matters; unfortunately, this service was not available at the time.

DEVELOPING SHARED THINKING

Facilitators initially helped Sadia to seek appropriate support for her health and housing problems, then they invited her to do a shared observation of Ayaan, based on carefully planning activities with specific toys that interested him (light, colour, sound and texture), as well as making a scrapbook to develop a shared sense of joy and wonder at her growing baby. This stepped intervention was individually tailored to support attunement.

Facilitators made concerted efforts to engage Sadia, and draw her out of what felt like a listless, trance-like state. Slowly it became possible for Sadia to begin to *take in* and develop trust in the facilitators, who conveyed, 'I thought about your baby, and I am interested in him and I am interested in you.' At a time when Sadia may have felt invisible and unlovable herself, facilitators showed her that she was worthy of positive attention.

PARALLEL PROCESS

Over time, it became possible for Sadia to come into clearer focus in reflective discussions, and this in turn helped her to bring Ayaan's needs into clearer focus. After Sadia had expressed her taboo feelings about her *greedy* baby, she could focus more on his needs.

Once facilitators had expressed their exasperation with Sadia, she became more visible in discussions and then facilitators were able to better connect to her. They were now able to bear Sadia's difficult emotions and abstain from judging her, and she could release these feelings without feeling compelled to act on her negative urges. Change became possible, as opposed to *forgetting* and *pushing their pain out of mind*, by just referring them onto another service. The facilitators' ability to hold in mind and tolerate the anxiety felt when initially seeing this dyad allowed them to develop a genuine, empathetic relationship with Sadia and Ayaan, who then became more animated.

FEAR OF MESS

Maleeha attended the group with her 18-month-old daughter, Shakira, a wide-eyed child with thick curls, dressed in frilled tutus with oversized bows on her head. Mother would warn her to stay away from mess and scolded, 'Shakira! I told you not to get messy; you look like a little tramp.' Maleeha's shrill and penetrating warnings grated on facilitators. They struggled to feel patient with her, and instead could only feel sympathy for Shakira, who appeared like a perfect little doll, who was to be admired but never played with.

REFLECTION – DEVELOPING EMPATHY TOWARDS MOTHERS

Facilitators initially thought Maleeha to be cruel and harsh towards her toddler; they felt frustrated and protective of Shakira. They dismissed Maleeha as uncaring and thoughtless (Davies and Ward 2011).

Once they were able to think that for Maleeha the mess represented a sense of being dangerously out of control, they began to understand that she needed a perfectly dressed child to demonstrate that she herself was coping. If Shakira appeared to be messy, as most happy children do during play, this might indicate that she was not doing enough as a mother to meet her basic needs of keeping her clean; she was terrified that her baby would be 'taken away from her'.

THE IMPACT OF STAFF KINDNESS AND
TOLERANCE ON MOTHER AND BABY

Gradually facilitators created manageable opportunities, such as hand painting, which allowed Shakira to play and get a little messy in a way that felt bearable for her mother. Maleeha was helped to see curiosity in Shakira as a way to learn about the world and appreciate the benefits of free play. She felt less ashamed and angry if her daughter did not look perfect. This change was visible as she became more relaxed within herself and her relationship with her toddler improved.

THE IMPORTANCE OF SUPERVISION: 'HOW DO MOTHER-BABY RELATIONSHIPS CHANGE?'

The discipline of spending reflective time after each group allowed facilitators to think about what each baby represented to their mother, as well as what they, the facilitators, may represent for the family. This helped them to understand some of the negative responses they received from teenage parents, who saw them initially as unhelpful authority figures they were rebelling against.

The challenge of meeting young parents on their wavelength, without being patronizing yet offering a safe adult presence without slipping into a maternal role, was ongoing, and discussed repeatedly. Facilitators then became able to attune more effectively to the often raw and painful needs of this group, and this atmosphere proved to be transformative for the mother and baby relationships, their families and communities.

CONCLUSION

Facilitators were surprised by the strength of emotions evoked by their work with mother baby groups. It could be tempting at times to believe that some people are, in fact, impossible to reach. Then hope is lost. The experience of facilitators showed that through the reflective practice described here, they were able to make themselves available both to reflect on their own responses to mothers and their babies in the groups, as well as to notice and hold onto hopeful moments, in sometimes extremely difficult, chaotic and changeable life circumstances, and vitally, to follow them up.

The reflective method helped them to facilitate groups in such a diverse community setting that allowed sustainable change to take place, and to contribute to the babies' developmental life chances. It allowed an exploration of the complex factors that underlie parents' and babies' behaviour. This enabled facilitators to attune to the authentic needs of the parent-baby couple. As parents were sometimes in severe emotional crisis, child protection considerations were always part of the reflective discussions (McBrien 2007; Ward, Brown and Westlake 2012).

The struggle for positive change for parents and babies from chronically deprived backgrounds with many complex social and mental health difficulties challenged facilitators' emotional capacity to their utmost. Hope was crucial to make this work possible, rather than viewing it without hope and seeing it as impossible.

The key to successful change when working with *hard to reach families*, as described here, was to provide conditions whereby facilitators had opportunities to reflect on their practice in a supportive, reflective group environment. This helped them to attune to families sufficiently to provide reparative experiences and to positively transform parents' relationships with their babies. It would be useful for organizations working with babies and families to be mandated to provide reflective practice groups, and thereby build organizational cultures that are inherently reflective.

REFERENCES

Bell, S. and Morse, S. (2005) 'Delivering sustainability therapy in sustainable development projects.' *Journal of Environmental Management 75*, 1, 37–51.

Brookfield, S. (1998) 'Critically reflective practice.' *Journal of Continuing Education in the Health Professions 18*, 4, 197–205.

Davies, C. and Ward, H. (2011) *Safeguarding Children across Services: Messages from Research*. London: Jessica Kingsley Publishers.

Fraiberg, S., Adelson, E. and Shapiro, V. (1975) 'Ghosts in the nursery.' *Journal of the American Academy of Child Psychiatry 14*, 3, 387–421.

Johns, C. and Burnie (2013) *Becoming a Reflective Practitioner*. 4th edn. New York: Wiley-Blackwell.

McBrien, B. (2007) 'Learning from practice – reflections on a critical incident.' *Accident and Emergency Nursing 15*, 3, 128–133.

Parker, C. (2015) 'NICE antenatal and postnatal mental health clinical guidelines.' *Progress in Neurology and Psychiatry 19*, 5, 4–5.

Schön, Donald A. (1983). *The Reflective Practitioner: How Professionals Think in Action.*
New York: Basic Books.
Ward, H., Brown, R. and Westlake, D. (2012) *Safeguarding Babies and Very Young
Children from Abuse and Neglect.* London: Jessica Kingsley Publishers.

CHAPTER 17

Empowering Professionals to Facilitate Parent-Baby Groups

Teaching Attunement

Monika Celebi and Catherine O'Keefe

This chapter draws on the experience of teaching early years professionals how to facilitate parent-baby and toddler groups. It describes elements of the training that have been found effective by participants and by trainers to convey and experience the concept of attunement in as many different ways as possible.

Inevitably each parent-baby and toddler group session is unique and a form of improvisation. Unexpected things always happen, which is why we do not believe in a one size fits all approach, but prefer to empower professionals to use themselves as a sounding board so they will be confident to relate to each parent, baby and toddler in their groups individually.

Theories from **group analysis** (Bion 2014; Foulkes and Anthony 1989), attachment research (Schore and Schore 1999), innate intersubjectivity (Nagy 2010; Stern 1985), Video Interaction Guidance (Kennedy, Landor and Todd 2011), mindfulness (Kabat-Zinn 2013) and movement therapy (Payne 1997) provide the theoretical and practical framework. The training promotes learning, which is reflective and experiential. It aims to be relevant to a range of different types of groups for parents, babies and toddlers as well as various styles of delivery.

BACKGROUND

The four-day training was developed by me (Monika Celebi) when I worked at the Oxford Parent Infant Project (OXPIP). It has been delivered over the last six years and so far has been attended by more than 170 early years professionals. The training has benefitted from the evaluations and feedback of participants, and co-facilitators Bobby Taylor, Catherine O'Keefe and Jan Tomlinson, all parent infant psychotherapists, who were also trained in Video Interaction Guidance (VIG).

AIMS

The overall aims of the training are:

- To observe and reflect on the psycho-physical responses evoked by being in a group, and by working with babies and toddlers.

- To notice anxiety and practise ways to manage anxiety.

- To learn about the impact of toxic stress on parents, babies, toddlers and facilitators, and how to nurture its opposite: a calm and connect system.

- To experience attunement via embodied **mentalization** and strength-based video feedback.

- To reflect on recurring themes, on the needs of parents, babies and toddlers, and on the role of the group facilitator.

KEY ELEMENTS OF THE TRAINING EXPERIENCE

CREATING AN AMBIENCE OF TRUST AND SAFETY

Lowering anxiety is a pre-requisite to thinking (Moberg 2011). Recognizing and managing one's stress response via the executive function of the brain (UNICEF 2014) is fundamental to working with groups of parents and babies, as babies (and groups) can raise profound anxieties in us all, as well as mobilize our care-taking systems (Panksepp and Biven 2007). 'I was nervous to begin with, but once we got started, I quickly felt at ease' (Sophia). Activating the calm and connect system is conducive to switching on the mammalian vagus (Celebi 2013; de Zulueta 2015; Porges 2011; Schore and Schore 1999), which is linked to regulation and to soothing.

In the training we model the creation of an ambience, a relaxed atmosphere in a friendly, benign environment. 'I was not sure about being in a group, but the trainers were welcoming and soon I felt we are all here for the same purpose' (Chloe). We want participants to feel comfortable, like being in a safe cave, or like being a baby in a snuggly, comfortable nest. Research tells us that when we feel safe, we can release feel-good hormones, which are conducive to learning (Celebi 2013; Moberg 2011). *Once participants experience the effects of a calm and connect system and understand our intention, they are better able to recreate such an atmosphere within their parent and baby and toddler groups.*

De Zulueta talks about 'primal empathy' (de Zulueta 2006), including non-verbal synchrony, like a subcortical (before thinking) emotional **resonance** between individuals (similar to attunement); it is conveyed via breathing patterns, quality of movement, use of personal space, facial expressions, eye contact and vocalization (tone of voice).

A GROUP CAN FUNCTION LIKE A SOOTHING CONTAINER

Soothing and regulating babies is the first task of any parent and a central theme of all parent-baby and toddler groups. Practising gentle, apparently simple, repetitive movements such as rocking and humming lullabies in a group can have a profound effect, with all participants connecting on a primitive level of togetherness, which strengthen the sense that the group is a benign container.

In the training these mechanisms are demonstrated, experienced by all and then thought about. Throughout we practise mindfulness exercises, such as pausing (at regular intervals) and 'being in the present moment', noticing breath, posture, and any recurring patterns of thoughts, feelings, judgements and behaviour. All these contribute to creating an environment that models a calm and connect system. We link the experience of self-regulation in the training environment to how facilitators can support parents to regulate their babies and toddlers in the groups they lead.

NON-VERBAL COMMUNICATION

Parents and babies communicate via sound, touch and gaze, therefore we explore these senses through various group activities, such as gentle touch, nursery rhymes, lullabies and rocking baby dolls. Engaging in these child-like activities creates a sense of playfulness and joy, which is amplified because it is shared in a group.

Touch exercises very quickly foster a sense of intimacy and trust. Discussions will name some of the difficult feelings touch can evoke, as well as reflect on the life-supporting qualities of deliberate, relational and sensitive touch and how important it is for babies' and toddlers' wellbeing.

Most important, though, is to notice what real babies and toddlers are like. This is done in the fishbowl practice.

THE FISHBOWL

Participants watch trainers lead a Therapeutic Touch–baby massage session in the format of a *fishbowl*. The trainers together with a group of real parents and real babies form an inner circle on the mat, with the training participants creating a second outer circle. Everyone says their name, to just hear their voice and acknowledge that all are, in some form, part of the big group in the room. *Participant observers* are invited to hum along with songs, and join in with some of the nursery rhymes and singing. They stroke their dolls to copy and learn from the parents. They are involved, and contribute to the overall ambience but are nevertheless one step removed.

Training participants thus have an opportunity to observe without responsibility, so they can notice their emotional responses to the interactions between parents and babies and the facilitators. Participants have said, 'Seeing mothers with their babies made me want to hold a baby too' (Gita); 'I was surprised about the pace and space, everyone was included, babies were equal members of the group' (Sherika).

Watching such a session in this format is likely to evoke profound feelings about babies, groups and attunement as well as mis-attunement. It inevitably also raises reflections on the desire to intervene and maybe make things better. This gives opportunities to discuss the **abstinence of the facilitator**.

The fishbowl session lends itself to discussions about the role of the facilitator and the complexity of interactions in all parent-baby groups and about how we can never predict, nor always get it right.

THE CONSTANTLY SHIFTING GROUP ENVIRONMENT

Any parent-baby and toddler group is full of curious, uninhibited babies and toddlers seeking responsiveness and wanting to engage. Parents will respond with their whole being, mould their body to comfort or bend down to match baby's height. They may crouch on the floor to play, or even lie down or roll about. The movement aspect is central because babies do not stay still for long, unless they are asleep, and their needs are immediate. Similarly the group facilitator will use all of herself, body, face and tone of voice, heart and mind to interact with each and every individual in the group. There is no one blueprint, other than recognizing that each group creates its own dance of constantly changing interactions.

EMBODIED MENTALIZATION

We all communicate via embodied mentalization (Shai and Belsky 2011). This process through which we attune to others is at the heart of our work. Facilitators often sense what is happening in their whole body, before they can think and name it. In a similar manner parents intuit their baby's needs. This process precedes verbalization. The next step is to find words to further enhance mentalization and encourage mind-minded behaviour (Fonagy, Gergely and Jurist 2005; Meins *et al.* 2011). *Babies function at a preverbal level, therefore helping parents to attune to their babies is the most basic task, which underlies all work within parent-baby groups.*

To encourage training participants to feel with their body and their mind, we ask them to hold a baby doll for a whole day. We have found that responses range from the desire to hug, to the memory of one's own babies. After a few hours, we can usually also notice the desire to put the doll down or *get rid* of it. These are opportunities to reflect on one's own personal experiences, as well as on the ambivalence evoked by looking after vulnerable babies, even though we are only dealing with dolls. Thinking about the themes in parent-baby groups draws on our own experiences as a baby, and as a parent, and on all our prior work with parents and babies. Feelings evoked by parent-baby groups can be raw and benefit from subsequent reflection with a co-facilitator and in supervision.

THE CONSTANT DANCE OF RECIPROCITY – IDENTIFYING MOMENTS OF ATTUNEMENT ON VIDEO

We discuss ideas of innate intersubjectivity (Nagy 2010), namely, that newborn babies adjust their behaviours according to the responsiveness of their interaction partner, and are extremely sensitive and able to detect and react to communication disturbances. We watch film clips where we can see reciprocity (Stern 1985; Trevarthen 1985; UNICEF 2014), the *serve and return* between parent and baby. Together we look for the source of initiatives: is the parent following the baby/toddler, intruding or ignoring? We notice different channels of verbal and non-verbal communication, such as pacing, rhythm, tone of voice, body posture and movement qualities.

From here we progress to look at the different links made between parents and babies in the groups, and how often, when we slow the video down, we can see that all group participants, adults and babies, move and vocalize not in unison, but in tune with each other, with unconscious awareness of each other's presence at all times. This reinforces the notion that usually most of us are unconsciously attuning to others, and only notice something is amiss when this attunement is absent.

WATCH, WAIT AND WONDER

Watch, Wait and Wonder (WWW) is an approach to teaching attunement that was developed originally by Nancy Cohen *et al.* (1999) and further extended by others (Celebi 2014; Zilibowitz n.d.). It suggests a slowing down, giving space and being curious before intervening.

We use role play where participants literally step into a parent's or baby's/toddler's shoes in a pretend Watch, Wait and Wonder situation, where the pretend parents are asked to follow their pretend baby's lead for five minutes. This can be a challenge for some, who may tend to show and teach rather than sit back and wait. It can also bring much laughter and playfulness as participants are allowed to be and feel like a baby again. It is also a good starting point for reflecting on what it feels like to be a baby with a depressed parent, who is preoccupied and cannot attune.

We film the WWW exercise, look at best moments together and give participants strength-based feedback, based on the principles of attunement, interaction and guidance (PAIG). These are grounded in the observations of attuned interactions of animals and humans, in their natural environment (Kennedy, Landor and Todd 2015).

LEARNING BY DOING

The most challenging and most rewarding part of the training is for participants to set up and lead their own real-life parent-baby and toddler group in their place of work, which is filmed with the help of a friendly colleague. We then look at footage of the best interactions between facilitator and group members (adults and babies/toddlers) in small supervision groups. Evaluations repeatedly tell us that, in spite of initial reluctance, or shyness to be filmed, this is one of their most profound learning experiences.

VIDEO ENHANCED REFLECTIVE PRACTICE

Video enhanced reflective practice (VERP) is a way of supporting professionals by reflecting on filmed best moments of their day-to-day practice. Its theoretical base is Video Interaction Guidance (Kennedy *et al.* 2015). Each participant in turn shows footage of when they were attuned with mothers and babies in the groups they led. Being seen and told by others that they are doing the 'right thing' quite likely releases feel-good chemicals, which are sensed and shared by all who are present.

Watching herself leading a parent-baby and toddler group on screen, and focusing on moments of attunement and reciprocity, Renate said, 'I was surprised how everyone, mothers and babies, were included. I'm pleased with the impact I've had.'

The attuned images onscreen often contradict internal critical voices. This is also called **cognitive dissonance**. Beth said, 'I was flustered because so many things were going wrong. I felt I was going too fast, but when I watched it back on film it was the opposite, I looked relaxed and the babies were really quiet.' Beth discovered that she was more competent than she originally gave herself credit for: 'It helped that others pointed out to me what I did right, otherwise I could have easily just focused on my mistakes.' Starting with what worked well encouraged her to think of how to change and improve her practice further.

CONCLUSION

Time and again participants have fed back that their personal experience of attunement during the training aided them to understand themselves better: 'I loved the friendly atmosphere, I felt encouraged to experiment, and didn't worry about looking foolish' (Ronda). They felt enthused: 'I can't wait to start my own group,' is a common feedback comment.

Attunement is at the heart of parenting, and central to facilitating parent-baby and toddler groups. Teaching it challenges us to help professionals become aware of what we tend to do unconsciously and automatically. Noticing how and when we are attuned (or not) gives us a body-felt experience, which we can think about and then use consciously.

The elements of the training described in this chapter aim to support best practice of early years professionals leading groups for parents and babies and toddlers. Their personal relationships with each and every one of their group members contribute to *weaving the cradle*, and to looking out for the youngest in society.

REFERENCES

Bion, W.R. (2014) *Experiences in Groups, and Other Papers*. London: Routledge.

Celebi, M. (2013) 'Helping to reduce parental anxiety in the perinatal period.' *Journal of Health Visiting 1*, 8, 438–442.

Celebi, M. (2014) 'Baby watching: facilitating parent-infant interaction groups.' *Journal of Health Visiting 2*, 7, 362–367.

Cohen, N.J., Muir, E., Lojkasek, M., Muir, R., Parker, C.J., Barwick, M. and Brown, M. (1999) 'Watch, wait, and wonder: testing the effectiveness of a new approach to mother-infant psychotherapy.' *Infant Mental Health Journal 20*, 4, 429–451.

de Zulueta, F. (2006) *From Pain to Violence: The Traumatic Roots of Destructiveness*. 2nd edn. Chichester: John Wiley & Sons.

de Zulueta, F. (2015) *From Pain to Violence and How to Break the Cycle | Felicity de Zulueta | TEDxEastEnd. TEDx Talks*, 20 February 2015. Available at: https://youtu.be/8d2grzTn3M4 (Accessed: 8 December 2016).

Fonagy, P., Gergely, G. and Jurist, E. (2005) *Affect Regulation, Mentalization, and the Development of the Self*. New York: Other Press.

Foulkes, S.H. and Anthony, E.J. (1989) *Group Psychotherapy: The Psychoanalytic Approach*. 2nd edn. London: Karnac Books.

Kabat-Zinn, J. (2013) *Full Catastrophe Living: How to Cope with Stress, Pain and Illness Using Mindfulness Meditation*. London: Little, Brown.

Kennedy, H., Landor, M. and Todd, L. (eds) (2011) *Video Interaction Guidance: A Relationship-Based Intervention to Promote Attunement, Empathy and Wellbeing*. Philadelphia: Jessica Kingsley Publishers.

Kennedy, H., Landor, M. and Todd, L. (eds) (2015) *Video Enhanced Reflective Practice: Professional Development through Attuned Interactions*. London: Jessica Kingsley Publishers.

Meins, E., Fernyhough, C., de Rosnay, M., Arnott, B., Leekam, S.R. and Turner, M. (2011) 'Mind-mindedness as a multidimensional construct: appropriate and nonattuned mind-related comments independently predict infant-mother attachment in a socially diverse sample.' *Infancy 17*, 4, 393–415.

Moberg, K.U. (2011) *The Oxytocin Factor: Tapping the Hormone of Calm, Love, and Healing*. London: Pinter & Martin.

Nagy, E. (2010) 'The newborn infant: a missing stage in developmental psychology.' *Infant and Child Development 20*, 1, 3–19.

Panksepp, J. and Biven, L. (2007) *The Archaeology of Mind: Neuroevolutionary Origins of Human Emotions*. New York: W.W. Norton.

Payne, H. (1997) *Creative Movement and Dance in Groupwork (Creative Activities in Groupwork)*. Hove: Speechmark Publishing.

Porges, S.W. (2011) *The Polyvagal Theory: Neurophysiological Foundations of Emotions, Attachment, Communication, and Self-Regulation*. New York: W.W. Norton.

Schore, A.N. and Schore, S. (1999) *Affect Regulation and the Origin of the Self: The Neurobiology of Emotional Development*. Hillsdale, NJ: Lawrence Erlbaum Associates.

Shai, D. and Belsky, J. (2011) 'When words just won't do: introducing parental embodied mentalizing.' *Child Development Perspectives 5*, 3, 173–180.

Stern, D.N. (1985) *The Interpersonal World of the Infant: A View from Psychoanalysis and Developmental Psychology*. 14th edn. New York: Basic Books.

Trevarthen, C. (1985) 'Human developmental neuropsychology.' *Neuropsychologia 23*, 6, 815–816.

UNICEF (2014) *New Insights into Brain Development: A Conversation with Dr. Jack Shonkoff*. UNICEF, 24 April 2014. Available at: https://youtu.be/QvvZ98N6HsE (Accessed: 8 December 2016).

Zilibowitz, M. (n.d.) *Watch, Wait and Wonder: A Modified Version*. Available at: http://www.earlyyears.org.au/_data/assets/pdf_file/0017/155213/Zilibowitz_Michael.pdf (Accessed: 8 December 2016).

Final Thoughts

Monika Celebi

I am delighted you made it to this section of the book (or maybe you are starting here?).

During the process of editing, I have learned a tremendous amount about the many ways professionals run groups for parents, babies and toddlers with such good outcomes. I am fascinated by the variety of approaches, each valuable in its own right. These groups are all in place only because there are dedicated professionals working above and beyond the call of duty to make them happen. The stories they tell are mesmerizing, sometimes sad, often uplifting. They show that a little intervention can go a long way.

This book is a triumph of collaboration: the voices of 31 experts in the field of group work in the perinatal period from many different professional backgrounds, different countries, even continents, sharing their vast experience, because they know that families benefit and future unhappiness can be prevented or at least reduced.

We know the inevitable results of neglect and abuse in the early years. The social, emotional and financial cost of family breakdowns increases the risk of children going into care, developing mental health problems, turning to drugs and alcohol for self-medication, and becoming disenchanted with society, creating a general sense of hopelessness. The human and economic benefits of early interventions 'are likely to be more effective than reactive services and (in the long run) deliver economic and social benefits ' (WAVE Trust with Department for Education 2013, p.5).

Groups for parents, babies and toddlers cost relatively little. As Jocelyn Cornwell, Chief Executive of the Point of Care Foundation, points out: 'The way we care for the most vulnerable is indicative of the health of our society as a whole' (Cornwell 2015).

As we can see from the practitioners and authors in this book, time and again the allocated resources are woefully inadequate! Policy makers and commissioners need to act now. We require more funding for research and training, and above all investment to run groups for parents, babies and toddlers.

Groups have enormous potential to become supportive, healing communities for mothers, fathers and their babies and toddlers at a time of great change in their lives. I think that all expecting and new parents should have access to groups, appropriate for their needs, and wherever they may happen to live.

Every ending is also a new beginning. I hope you will be inspired and that you will use this book to help us weave the cradle in whatever way you can.

REFERENCES

Cornwell, J. (2015) 'How we care for the vulnerable is indicative of society's health.' *Nursing Times*, 18 November. Available at: https://www.nursingtimes.net/break-time/expert-opinion/how-we-care-for-the-vulnerable-is-indicative-of-societys-health/7000212.article (Accessed: 8 December 2016).

WAVE Trust in collaboration with Department for Education (2013) *Conception to Age 2 – The Age of Opportunity. Addendum to the Government's Vision for the Foundation Years: 'Supporting Families in the Foundation Years'*. Available at: http://www.wavetrust.org/our-work/publications/reports/conception-age-2-age-opportunity (Accessed: 1 December 2016).

Glossary

Abstinence of the facilitator Recognizing the strong urge we all have to engage with babies and toddlers and the fine line a group facilitator treads when being responsive, but not taking initiatives to satisfy their own desires (to hug or play with a baby, for instance), which may undermine the parent.

Baby bonding champions Mothers asked to coordinate the efforts of the workshop participants and extend the work in their communities. They are identified because they are loving, gentle and playful with their babies, clearly recapped teaching points and were friendly towards others. Every six months, they attend a Lullaby Africa training session, to share their successes, and receive more information on attachment and play.

Clinical hexagon An image of the multiple aspects a group supervisor has to think about: the organizational context, the **dynamic administration**, the group process, the group members and in particular the group member, who is presenting; the client, dyad or group, which is being brought for consideration; and the supervisor's own self and observation of their own feelings and responses during the supervision session.

Cognitive dissonance A term coined by Festinger (1957) to describe a jarring of beliefs and assumptions. For example, when there is a conflict between feeling like a failure as a parent or facilitator and seeing oneself at successful moments on video, or receiving strength-based feedback about yourself from others. Then there is an opportunity to make adjustments, because we have an innate tendency to reduce such dissonance.

Containment The way one person can hear and bear the difficult and distressing feelings of another, and 'reframe' them so they feel much more manageable. A parent can tolerate a baby's upset and therefore help make it better. A facilitator comprehends the emotional content expressed in the group and this helps all to keep equilibrium.

Creative process A process of experimentation through which creative ideas and expression are communicated.

Dynamic administration Covers all activities the facilitator performs to set up and hold the group setting: establishing a relationship with each group member prior to the group, providing a suitable setting, clarifying time boundaries, receiving and responding to messages from group members, including the need for extra attention around the ending of a group. These all have significance for members, and understanding their meaning supports the group's sense of security.

Explicit communication The clear way in which activities are used to help parents experience different approaches to interacting. Parents are aware of the aim of activities set up to support communications skills.

Group analysis A form of group therapy where the group itself is seen as the therapeutic agent. The therapy is 'by the group of the group including the conductor'. 'Conductor' is used in preference to 'leader' to reflect a more democratic process.

Implicit communication The way in which the group models interaction as 'live' experiences of attuned interaction. This is the 'ethos' or way of being within the Baby Steps programme.

Kinaesthetic empathy Attuning to a person's affective state through embodied mentalization and movement.

Mammalian vagus Part of the autonomic nervous system unique to mammals, linked to social engagement via eye contact, facial expression and vocalization, also connected to the heart and to digestion. It is stimulated in a peaceful and safe environment, which allows comfort, empathy, feeling and some thinking.

These are experienced in a body-felt way and can be discovered through reflection and mindfulness. Positive experiences and interactions will occur in such an attuned environment.

Mentalization The parental capacity to experience their baby as an individual with their own personality traits, strengths and sensitivities. Parents who mentalize are able to adopt a curious approach to imagine what the baby may be experiencing and feeling. They can also reflect on their own feelings and think how this might affect the baby.

Mentalization-based treatment (MBT) An evidence-based intervention for treating borderline personality disorder (BPD) (Bateman and Fonagy 2006).

Mirroring A group allows the members to catch a glimpse of themselves, or part of themselves (often a repressed part), reflected in the interaction of other group members and thereby recognize something in themselves they may not be aware of. Each member is thereby better able to understand the effect they have on, and how they are seen by, others. Foulkes (1984) coined the term the 'hall of mirrors' as a metaphor for the enhanced mirroring, which takes place in groups.

Parallel process The supervision group can mirror and reflect the dynamic of the mother and baby group or some aspect of it and may be able to observe this and find out something new.

Open discussion group A steady support group for parents aiming at empowering them in their parenting role. This group does not have an agenda for discussion.

Parent-baby and toddler cooking group Multi-family group intervention aiming at promoting positive interaction between mothers and youngsters through cooking. Members may be of diverse cultural backgrounds.

Parentese A universal way of speaking to babies, using a higher pitch and slower rhythm with shorter phrases, leaving pauses so the baby can respond.

Parent-toddler group Multi-family group intervention aiming at supporting families throughout toddlerhood (one to three years old), based on the Anna Freud Centre's 'parent-toddler groups'.

Polyvagal contagion Our unconscious reaction to the state of excitement in another person. Our nervous system responds to the neurophysiological state of people, to their state of excitement or relaxation, both reflexive expressions of the nervous system. A fight-or-flight reaction makes us literally see red and become, tense, suspicious and on guard. According to de Zulueta (2016), being in the green zone is the opposite state, which allows for a relaxation of defences and a switching on of the **mammalian vagus** and the care-taking system. All of these non-verbal processes are enhanced by the babies and they affect all group members in some way.

Primary intersubjectivity Face-to-face interaction between two people, where emotions are expressed and perceived in a two-way dialogue and body language, hand movements, eyes, voice tones and facial expressions all combine in a synchronized communicative 'dance'.

Psychological mindedness According to the *Psychodynamic Diagnostic Manual*, this is 'an individual's ability to observe and reflect on his or her own internal life' (PDM Task Force 2006, p.82).

Reflective functioning The capacity to imagine mental states in oneself and others. For parents and carers, it involves adopting a curious approach and wondering about a baby's behaviour and what this might mean in terms of the baby's experience and feelings. Through this capacity for reflection, parents and carers come to understand their own behaviour and responses, the behaviour and responses of others and how these interact and intertwine. Parents who take a reflective approach are able to mentalize.

Repetition compulsion Freud described this as when a person is compelled to repeat elements of an earlier conflictual relationship.

A mother might unconsciously repeat with her own baby aspects of what went wrong in her own mothering.

Resonance This happens when background experiences are roused in current ones. Someone else's story may strike a chord with the listener and remind them consciously or unconsciously of a personal experience. They may become more aware of feelings they initially were not aware of and this makes it possible for difficult feelings to find clearer communication.

Secondary intersubjectivity Attuned communication between two people involving a shared focus on an object or activity. This develops in the second half of an infant's first year and is seen, for example, when an infant looks from a toy or item of food to their parent for their response and back again.

Secure base Mary Ainsworth (1982) coined this term to describe how a child feels with a secure attachment figure, and the idea has been extended. Children will seek a parent and adults whom they trust, who help them to feel calm enough to think, to share companionable interactions and pleasure. Adults too seek out a secure base if they feel threatened, ill or exhausted.

Sensitive caregiving Requires moment-by-moment attunement with the baby's needs, emotions and intentions, and an ability to mentalize.

Therapeutic space The provision of a safe, confidential and permissive space where client and therapist may explore emerging psychological material.

Watch, Wait and Wonder A child-led psychotherapeutic approach, which uses the child's spontaneous activity in a free play format to enhance maternal sensitivity and responsiveness. The child and parent work through developmental and relational struggles through play. Central to this process is engaging the parent to be reflective about the child's inner world of feelings, thoughts and desires.

REFERENCES

Ainsworth, M. (1982) 'Attachment Retrospect and Prospect.' In C.M. Parkes and J. Stevenson-Hinde (eds) *The Place of Attachment in Human Behavior*. London: Tavistock.

Bateman, A.W. and Fonagy, P. (2006) *Mentalization-Based Treatment for Borderline Personality Disorder: A Practical Guide*. Oxford: Oxford University Press.

de Zulueta, F. (2016) Personal communication. 13 July.

Festinger, L. (1957) *A Theory of Cognitive Dissonance*. Stanford, CA: Stanford University Press.

Foulkes, S.H. (1984) *Therapeutic Group Analysis*. London: Maresfield Reprints.

PDM Task Force (2006) *Psychodynamic Diagnostic Manual*. Silver Spring, MD: Alliance of Psychoanalytic Organizations.

Useful Resources

The Anna Freud Centre runs short courses, training and workshops in infant mental health, parent infant psychotherapy, and working with parents and babies in groups.
www.annafreud.org

The Association of Dance Movement Psychotherapy UK (ADMP UK) is the professional organization for Dance Movement Psychotherapy in the UK.
http://admp.org.uk

The Association for Psychodynamic Practice and Counselling in Organisational Settings (APPCIOS) provides accreditation, validation and a professional network for psychodynamic practitioners working within organizational settings in a variety of professional roles in the UK.
http://appcios.com

The Association of Video Interaction Guidance UK (AVIGuk) is the organization that regulates standards in the quality of Video Interaction Guidance in the UK. The website provides information on training, application, research and how to find a guider.
http://www.videointeractionguidance.net

The Begin Before Birth website has videos and materials on the impact of the antenatal period on all aspects of the baby's life.
www.beginbeforebirth.org

Getting to know...Your Baby videos is an app, developed by Angela Underdown, promoting emotional wellbeing before and after birth.
www.your-baby.org.uk

Harvard Center on the Developing Child has video, presentations and written information on the importance of early childhood and interventions that support babies and parents.
http://developingchild.harvard.edu/

Lighthouse Training runs short courses including the assessment and treatment of families in which severe child abuse and neglect has occurred or is at risk of occurring, perinatal mental health and mentalizing skills.
http://lighthouseparenting.net

Lullaby Africa is a charity that helps traumatized and disadvantaged mothers, fathers and carers in Kenya and Uganda to bond and form a healthy, natural attachment with their babies and toddlers.
www.lullabyafrica.org

Mellow Parenting offers training in Mellow Bumps and Mellow Babies on a regular basis in the UK and overseas.
www.mellowparenting.org

Parent Infant Partnership UK (PIPUK) is a charity committed to raising awareness of the 1001 Critical Days and to supporting the development of specialist therapeutic services that focus on the relationship between baby and parents where this might be at risk in order to enhance the wellbeing and future development of the child.
http://www.pipuk.org.uk

Contributors

Eleni Agathonos PhD is a psychologist, social worker and expert in child protection. She designed and initiated the VIMA programme and is one of the main scientific interdisciplinary committee members for the VIMA programme.

Gerry Byrne is head of attachment and perinatal services in Oxford Health NHS Trust. He is a tutor on the psychoanalytic observational studies course (Tavistock), an MBT trainer and supervisor (Anna Freud National Centre). Working with severe parenting breakdown for over 26 years, he innovated and leads on the Lighthouse© MBT-Parenting Programme within the FASS and ReConnect services.

Monika Celebi is a Video Interaction guider and supervisor and on the board of AVIGuk. She also trained and worked as a movement therapist, psychoanalytic psychotherapist, parent infant psychotherapist, yoga teacher, baby massage instructor and antenatal educator. She has pioneered training for facilitators of parent-baby groups and is a member of the Association for Psychodynamic Practice and Counselling in Organisational Settings .

Lisa Clayden has worked as a community midwife in East Oxford for eight years. She co-facilitates the Saplings project, which aims to provide extra support and comprehensive, joined-up care for some of the most vulnerable women in the area. She has a specialist interest in breastfeeding support.

Lynnaire Doherty is Māori (Ngati Porou and Ngapuhi iwi/tribes). Her background is as an early childhood education teacher, and psychologist. She established a kaupapa Māori trust to offer holistic support to families across Auckland. The service model includes culturally adapted Hoki ki te Rito-Oranga Whānau programmes based on Mellow Parenting.

Caroline Feltham-King works as an educational psychologist for Hampshire Children's Services, focusing on supporting parents, carers and educators of traumatized children in and from the care system. She is a supervisor and practitioner of Video Interaction Guidance. She has so far made three trips to Kenya with Lullaby Africa.

Rebecca Foster has been an educator for 37 years, specializing in teaching English to adults and to Speakers of Other Languages (ESOL). She has facilitated communication and parenting skills classes for hard to reach communities in children's centres and schools in rural situations.

Cristina Franklin originally trained as a nursery nurse and has subsequently attained a degree in Early Childhood Education and the NPQICL in Integrated Centre Leadership. She has worked extensively within the area of child and family support and has a particular passion for supporting families who have experienced domestic abuse.

Margaret Gallop is an independent group analytic psychotherapist. She contributes to the Oxford Parent Infant Project Parent Infant Training and psychodynamic training in higher education. She sees individuals, groups and supervisees in different settings. She co-convenes the IGA Diploma 'Using the group as a medium for supervision'.

Klio Geroulanou PhD is a clinical psychologist who has worked in multiple clinical as well as research settings, involving adults and children. Together with Katerina Ydraiou, she facilitated the first 18 months of VIMA's initiation and development. She is currently working as an external supervisor for PhD and MPhil students at Bolton University, New York College, Athens.

Sarah Haddow studied Dance Movement Psychotherapy (DMP) at Dance Voice, Bristol. She has been working with a charity founded to support children and adults using DMP. She is engaged with the Living Theory multi-professional research group in Bath, and a leading practitioner supporting mothers with postnatal depression in Somerset and Bristol.

Korina Hatzinikolaou works in the fields of developmental psychology and developmental psychopathology. She is Assistant Professor, School of Early Childhood Education, at Aristotle University of Thessaloniki, Greece, and the Scientific Coordinator of the Greek NGO One Child, One World. Her research and clinical practice focus on infant mental health and early intervention.

Tamara Hussain has worked with children and their families for more than 15 years in schools, nurseries and children's centres. She is interested in the emotional world of the child, and particularly enjoys working with adolescent mothers, supporting attachment relationships to develop.

Jessica James is a group analyst working as a parent infant psychotherapist and group specialist at the Anna Freud Centre Parent Infant Project, as well as training and supervising. For many years she ran groups at the Women's Therapy Centre and she continues to work independently running yoga, birth and baby groups in Hackney.

Camille Kalaja is originally from France. She has worked at the Leys children's centre in Oxford as a maternity outreach worker since April 2007 and collaborates with midwives, health visitors and other partner agencies. She supports families during pregnancy and after birth by leading groups for parents and babies, providing breastfeeding group and one-to-one support.

Gabrielle Lees is an art therapist and child and adolescent psychotherapist. She works in a specialist safeguarding service and a perinatal parent infant project in Oxford. She teaches at the Anna Freud Centre and on the Oxford MA in Psychoanalytic Infant Observation, is a national trainer for the Solihull Approach, and co-developed the Lighthouse© MBT-Parenting Programme.

Moira McCutcheon PhD, has over 24 years' experience working clinically in the NHS CAMHS, as a consultant child psychotherapist and as a head of psychotherapy. Her special interest is developing multi-disciplinary outreach services for the under fives in multi-ethnic communities. She consults to Local Authority court assessments, contact and family services.

Bridget Macdonald is a retired learning and development consultant at the Children and Young People's Services in Suffolk. She has 30 years' experience in social work practice and education, with a special interest in mothers and babies. She is an advanced supervisor with AVIGuk following seven years spent developing VIG in a cluster of Sure Start children's centres.

Rachel Moody is Head of Psychology at King Edward VI School, Southampton, an examiner for A level Psychology and co-author of three A level Psychology textbooks. She is a trustee of Lullaby Africa.

Myrto Nielsen is a psychologist, psychotherapist and child psychologist, and one of the main scientific interdisciplinary committee members for the VIMA programme.

Catherine O'Keefe originally trained as an art therapist and has worked across different client groups including adults with mental health problems and vulnerable children. She has trained as a parent infant psychotherapist and worked for the Oxford Parent Infant Project alongside maintaining an independent practice as a clinical supervisor and art therapist working with children.

Caryn Onions is Consultant Child and Adolescent Psychotherapist at the Mulberry Bush School near Oxford, and a supervisor and trainer for the Oxford Parent Infant Project. She consults to other professionals working in the field of infant, child and adolescent mental health.

Ruth Price is a Registered Dance Movement Psychotherapist, clinical supervisor and lecturer on the Masters in Dance Movement Psychotherapy course at Dance Voice, Bristol. Creativity and dance have been constant keys to freedom and wholeness in a career involving nursing, community dance and teaching. She is the founder of the Eve project.

Christine Puckering is a psychologist with a particular interest in very early relationships and how these can be supported when families are under stress. She is Programme Director for Mellow Parenting. She was awarded a Winston Churchill Foundation Travelling Fellowship, an Andrea Leadsom award and the Dilys Daws award for Infant Mental Health.

Penny Rackett is an educational psychologist working for East Lothian Council, an advanced supervisor in Video Interaction Guidance and a committee member of the Association of Infant Mental Health. She has a passion for supporting infants and their families in the early years.

Sheila Ritchie is a psychoanalytic psychotherapist and group analyst and works in an NHS Perinatal Mental Health Service. She teaches for the Anna Freud Centre and is Consultant Group Analyst in an NHS psychotherapy department. In private practice she sees individuals, couples and groups and supervises in a range of settings.

Marina Rova is a Dance Movement Psychotherapist and researcher based in London. Her clinical practice includes adult mental health, perinatal and family services and older adults living with dementia. She recently completed her practice-based doctorate research at the University of Roehampton investigating 'kinaesthetic empathy'.

Rachel Tainsh is a Chartered Physiotherapist. Within Mellow Parenting, she is particularly involved in projects for parents with learning disabilities and parents of children with disabilities. This also extends to work overseas to promote family integration and deinstitutionalization for children with disabilities, including in Moldova and Tajikistan.

Bobby Taylor has worked as a parent infant therapist for the last 14 years. She has a background in nursing, health visiting and psychodynamic counselling. She is a VIG guider and trainee supervisor. She has facilitated groups for parents and babies for many years as a way to supporting them in the early months of their relationship.

Norma Thompson has been involved with the provision of services for children since 1983. She has a degree in Early Childhood and in Educational Studies and an NPQICL in Integrated Centre Leadership. Her interest is in creating a shared vision with other professionals in developing services through continuous connections and joint training opportunities.

Angela Underdown PhD was an Associate Professor and Deputy Director of Warwick Infant and Family Wellbeing Unit. Angela is a Video Interaction Guidance supervisor. She authored the 'Getting to know...Your Baby videos', the NSPCC's Baby Steps perinatal programme, and many other publications. She recently trained 300 Infant Mental Health champions nationally.

Katerina Ydraiou is an MSc psychologist and family therapist. She has worked in a range of community clinical settings, both for adults as well as for children. Since 2013 she has been working in developing and establishing the VIMA programme. Her clinical interests and practice focus on prevention and early intervention.

Subject Index

Author Index